THE 7 VITAL SELF-CHECK HEALTH PROGRAM

ARE YOU FEELING LOST? IT'S TIME TO ADAPT TO HABITS THAT WILL UNBLOCK: FAILING RELATIONSHIPS, SELF-LOVE, AND SELF-DISCIPLINE TO ACHIEVE GOOD VIBES FOR A FULFILLING LIFESTYLE

JONRY HEYCE

© **Copyright 2021 - All rights reserved.**

The content contained within this book may not be reproduced, duplicated, or transmitted without direct written permission from the author or the publisher.

Under no circumstances will any blame or legal responsibility be held against the publisher, or author, for any damages, reparation, or monetary loss due to the information contained within this book, either directly or indirectly.

Legal Notice:

This book is copyright protected. It is only for personal use. You cannot amend, distribute, sell, use, quote or paraphrase any part, or the content within this book, without the consent of the author or publisher.

Disclaimer Notice:

Please note the information contained within this document is for educational and entertainment purposes only. All effort has been executed to present accurate, up-to-date, reliable, complete information. No warranties of any kind are declared or implied. Readers acknowledge that the author is not engaged in the rendering of legal, financial, medical, or professional advice. The content within this book has been derived from various sources. Please consult a licensed professional before attempting any techniques outlined in this book.

By reading this document, the reader agrees that under no circumstances is the author responsible for any losses, direct or indirect, that are incurred as a result of the use of the information contained within this document, including, but not limited to, errors, omissions, or inaccuracies.

CONTENTS

Introduction   5

1. BELIEVING IN YOUR ABILITY TO INFLUENCE YOUR LIFE   13
   What Is Self-Efficacy?   14

2. SOURCES OF SELF-BELIEF   25

3. THE PROCESS OF SELF-CONCILIATION   55
   What Is Self-Conciliation?   55
   The Self-Construal Theory   56

4. FACING OUR FEARS   70
   Assertiveness   70
   Aggressiveness versus Assertiveness   72
   What Prevents Assertiveness?   72
   Why is Assertiveness Important?   76
   How to Become More Assertive   80
   Fear   84
   Fear Management   86

5. FACE YOUR FEAR AND DISCOVER WHO YOU WANT TO BECOME   97
   Self-Esteem and Facing your Fears   97
   Self-Efficacy and Dealing with Your Fears   103
   Mental Resilience   103
   Self-Confidence   105
   Bad Habits   107
   Negative Emotions   109

6. THE POWER OF CONSTRUCTIVE RELATIONSHIPS 117
   What Are Constructive Relationships? 118
   Inclusion of Other in Self Theory 122
   Relationships and Decision-Making 124
   Familial and Social Support 129
   Social Mimicry and You 131
   The Golden Rule 135

7. THE NEW ME 137
   Overthinking: You Aren't Your Thoughts 139
   Self-Love: Unlock Your Best Life 142
   Self-Discipline 149

   Conclusion 157
   References 161

INTRODUCTION

"You are essentially who you choose to be, and everything that occurs in your life is to shape who you decide to become."

— BY JONRY HEYCE

Did you know that you have the power to transform your life to achieve good vibes and fulfillment? You may not think you have that power now, but when you're done reading this book, you will realize that you do, and that you have had it all along. Sayings like 'You are the master of your own universe' and 'You can change your stars' have been thrown about in conversation so often that they have become cliche. They are still frequently used today, and do you know why that is? Fads and trends come and go, but when there is truth in something, it sticks around. These sayings are still around because they are based on truth: the truth that you have the power and ability to create the life you really want for yourself.

How do you discover the strength that lies within you to overcome the worst fears in your life? The key to unlocking this inner strength, living the life you truly want, and becoming the person you want to be is acknowledging and understanding that you already have everything you need to create the best possible version of yourself. You.

You, and you alone, have the innate capacity to develop yourself. However, you, and only you, can also stand in your own way. How do you develop yourself today to become a better person than you were yesterday? Success in any area of life can be strongly linked to opportunity and timing but you can create opportunities for yourself at any given time. How do you achieve self-made success?

The answers to these questions may be simpler than you think, and this book is going to give them to you.

Think about success for a moment. What does it mean to you? Now, think about what has shaped your idea of success. Are you defining success for yourself or are you defining success based on what others tell you it is? Success comes in all shapes and sizes and can be defined differently in terms of your career, relationships, and other aspects of life.

Yes, your background, the society you live in, and your life experiences all influence your success, your interpersonal relationships, and how things manifest themselves in your life. However, those are not the only determinants. The biggest determinant for success in every part of your life lies within you.

That nagging, lingering feeling that you are lacking something in life can become immensely frustrating. You may even feel powerless to achieve the good vibes you are striving for. This thing that you lack, you can feel its impact on your happiness, your interpersonal relationships with others, and your overall wellbeing. You think you are doing everything right in life, so why don't you feel fulfilled? What is it that you are missing and stopping you from having the life you really want?

This book is based on scientific and psychological research coupled with my own knowledge and expertise as a health studies graduate and clinical adviser. It has been written to provide you with a clear understanding of human nature to bring you practical, actionable solutions to help you develop yourself and create the fulfilling life you so desperately want.

Do you feel you are ready for change and feel the strong urge to make that change happen to lead a life full of good vibes? Now is the time to take action and start making that happen. I will provide you with the 7 Vital Self-Check Health Program, including:

- The ability to influence your own life.
- The sources of self-belief and self-efficacy.
- The benefits of self-belief.
- The process of self-conciliation.
- How to face your fears and overcome them.
- The power of constructive relationships and how to create them.
- How to discover and shape a whole new you that you can be proud of.

If changing careers, starting your own business, or rekindling failed or failing relationships is one of your concerns, you have picked up the right book. You will gain valid self-awareness, self-motivation, discipline, confidence, and the determination to transform your life into what you want it to be.

ABOUT THE AUTHOR

I am a clinical advisor working for the NHS with 15 years of experience in the field of healthcare. My passion is fashion design, and my dream has always been to become a fashion designer. Since I am writing a book about achieving success and fulfillment in your life, why didn't I realize my dream? The answer is simple. While studying fashion design at college, others convinced me that achieving anything in the fashion industry in the UK was impossible because I lacked prominent connections. Due to the influence of others' opinions which created that conviction, I decided to change my path and aspirations from fashion to healthcare. It was easy to do because I already had a part-time job in a hospital as a healthcare assistant.

I gained a vast amount of knowledge about human nature and nurture during the pursuit of my first degree in BA Hons Health Studies at De Montfort University Leicester. I found this so fascinating that it sparked a keen interest in human behavior and personality traits. I came to understand human cognition and why people behave the way they do.

My second degree is a BSc Hons in Adult Nursing from Coventry University. Since acquiring this degree, I have met a variety of people with real physical, mental, and emotional problems. I find it incredibly satisfying and rewarding to assist others who are vulnerable and help them feel better. However, my biggest challenge is meeting people who have incurable conditions and are desperate for help, but there is not much a healthcare professional can do to improve their health. It is those people who are at a point where they cannot help themselves whatsoever. Many times, I see patients literally losing their lives when I can only do so much to assist. The best I can do is give them tender, sympathetic end-of-life care. Provided appropriately, it is some of the best care you can give a patient. While many nurses find it fulfilling, it breaks my heart.

This is what led me to write this book; to help others help themselves. Remember, my dream was to become a fashion designer and now here I am working in healthcare. Don't get me wrong, I find healthcare very rewarding as a vocation, but deep inside I have always lived with a void created by not achieving my goal and realizing my dream.

For that reason, I turned to self-help books, research, and motivational speakers. Doing so has helped me realize that the best person to help me was myself. I have since opened up a shop on Amazon and on Etsy. I wrote this book because I am a people person. I do not want anybody to go through the frustration I went through after giving up my dream. I believed people when they told me that I will never make it in fashion. Had I known what I know now, I would have pursued a career in fashion and made a success of it. I was very passionate, but I did not know that I had what it takes to do what I want to do.

I want to help people learn to believe in themselves. I am here to encourage and teach you that you have all it takes to develop yourself. Do not quit and give up your dreams, whatever they may be. Do not settle for anything less than what you really want in life. You can make your dreams and desires a reality. It is never too late. The best thing is you have it all; you do not need to rely on anyone else to make it happen. What is holding you back is the lack of understanding of what hinders your motivation. You need to learn how to apply practical solutions to motivate yourself. Develop your life and achieve those important goals you have always dreamt of. You have it all. You can heal yourself and become the best person you want to be.

1

BELIEVING IN YOUR ABILITY TO INFLUENCE YOUR LIFE

Do you believe in yourself? More importantly, do you believe in your ability to 'change your stars?'

Self-belief is also known as perceived self-efficacy. It is an important aspect of the way you see yourself that has the power to shape how you act, speak, think, and feel. It is the driving force behind working to achieve the goals you set for yourself in life or your failures. Self-belief can be influenced by a number of things, but let's first take a look at what, exactly, self-efficacy is.

WHAT IS SELF-EFFICACY?

Researchers have worked for decades to pin down an exact definition of self-efficacy. Each definition draws a similar conclusion. The first person to put forward the idea of self-efficacy was Canadian American psychologist Albert Bandura. He originally defined self-efficacy as a person's own belief in their ability to carry out a task according to set standards. The notion of self-efficacy has since become one of psychology's most-studied concepts and has been similarly defined by others:

- In a 1996 study, Schunk and Pintrich put forward a definition of self-efficacy as being an individual's judgment regarding their capability to plan, strategize, and achieve scheduled assignments.
- Also in 1996, Shanmao and Haung suggested that self-efficacy is a person's perception of their own capabilities in carrying out a task they are assigned.
- In a study conducted by McCombs in 2001, self-

efficacy was referred to as a student's belief in their own ability to carry out a task.
- In 2001 Schunk defined self-efficacy as an individual's beliefs about their own ability to either learn or perform tasks according to predetermined standards.

As you can see, various researchers have tried to further clarify Bandura's original concept of self-efficacy.

Why has this concept become so vital in psychology and education? Bandura suggested that self-belief determines how one thinks, feels, and behaves. It also determines a person's motivation to do or accomplish things, and therefore, their goals in life. This notion has since been further researched and proven to be true. Determining how we think, behave, and feel influences our perception of our place in this world.

My personal experience: In my early teen years, I believed that I was able to complete my education and become a fashion designer as a goal in my life. Being a designer was my dream. My belief in myself and my ability to make that dream come true reflected my positive self-efficacy. The way I thought, felt, and behaved was a major determining factor for where I am today.

Perceived Self-Efficacy

Perceived self-efficacy is your own personal belief in your ability to succeed at and accomplish something. It is not necessarily a true reflection of your capabilities, but rather what you think you can and cannot do. Whether or not you really can or cannot do something is irrelevant according to perceived self-efficacy. This greatly affects your life. If you believe that you cannot do something, you won't have the motivation to even give it a try.

Your personal beliefs about yourself influence important processes.

- *Cognitive:* The thought processes involved in acquiring, organizing, and using information.
- *Affective:* The processes that regulate how you emotionally react to things and regulation of different emotional states.

- *Motivation:* The choice of what action to take, taking that action, how much effort you put in, and whether you persist or not.
- *Self-regulation:* How your thought processes, motivation, behavioral patterns, and emotional state are shaped.

My personal experience: As an aspiring fashion designer, my positive self-belief is what led me to start the journey of becoming one. I believed that I could do it irrespective of whether I had the capabilities or not. This belief prompted me to apply at and attend a college, pursuing my dream. If I didn't believe I could achieve this goal, I wouldn't have even started my journey. If you don't start the journey toward achieving your dream, there is no possible way you can reach your goal.

What Is the Importance of Self-Efficacy?

> *"Having a healthy perceived self-esteem helps you think about yourself highly; the way you feel, speak and act, will lead to a super you and you will change the world."*
>
> — (KING, 2018)

Self-efficacy plays a vital role in your success in life, whether it is personal life, relationships, or your professional life. Self-belief permeates every aspect of your life and may even ultimately influence your personality. If you have poor self-efficacy beliefs, you're going to feel poorly about yourself. Feeling poorly about yourself may lead to developing a naturally negative disposition; negativity often begets more negativity. Your thoughts influence your emotions and your emotions, in turn, affect your actions. It can be seen as a chain reaction of internal events that become externally expressed. Those with poorly perceived self-efficacy have a tendency to avoid challenges wherever possible, believing they won't be able to overcome them. They have a higher likelihood of failure due to the influence their low self-efficacy has on their actions and may end up falling well short of realizing their full potential.

Positive self-efficacy, on the other hand, leads to a positive view of yourself, and you will therefore feel good about yourself. Your personality may naturally be positive and cause you to look on the positive side of life, even when faced with great challenges. People who have positively perceived self-efficacy are less likely to shy away from challenges and are more likely to be driven to succeed and accomplish their goals.

Another effect perceived self-efficacy has on your life is determining how you face challenges and take action to achieve your goals in life. Approaching life with a positive sense of self-efficacy and having a 'sunnier' disposition may aid in your problem-solving skills because you believe you can succeed, and therefore will find ways to do so. However, poor self-efficacy and approaching life with a negative outlook may weaken your problem-solving skills. You don't believe you can succeed, and therefore may be less inclined to be inventive and creative in finding ways to achieve goals and overcome challenges.

Ask yourself these questions to determine whether you have positive perceived self-efficacy.

- Do you see challenges as something you must overcome or a task or skill you must master?
- Do you have a higher level of commitment to the activities you take part in and your personal interests?
- Do you have a greater interest in the activities you take part in?
- Are you able to recover from disappointment or setbacks well; can you 'get back on the horse' quicker and more easily?

If you are able to answer 'yes' to these self-efficacy questions, chances are you have positively perceived self-efficacy and believe you can do anything you set your mind to.

Characteristics of those with poorly perceived self-efficacy include:

- Do you avoid challenges whenever possible?

- Do you focus on your personal failures?
- Do you focus on the negative outcomes of previous failures and the potential negative outcomes of future tasks?
- Have you got a strong belief that you will fail in endeavors and tasks because they are beyond your self-perceived scope of capability?
- Do you quickly and easily become discouraged and lose your confidence in what you are capable of in the face of setbacks and disappointment?

If you answered 'yes' to any of the above poor perceived self-efficacy questions, it may be time to stand back, take stock of the realities, and work on your perceived self-efficacy.

Self-efficacy extends beyond how you perceive your abilities. It plays a pivotal role in how you make decisions and plan your life in both personal and professional spheres. Holding your capabilities in high regard may lead to making decisions leading to reaching your goals and accomplishing tasks, despite the potential obstacles you may face having made that decision. Again, this ties in with having better problem-solving skills. Making decisions that bring you face-to-face with challenges develops keen problem-solving skills. It makes you believe you can and must overcome obstacles. You will learn to think in ways that will help you creatively tackle future tasks based on previous experience.

When your perceived self-efficacy is low, you avoid challenges by making decisions that have the least likelihood of encountering obstacles. When you don't have to face obstacles and find ways to overcome them, you don't learn to think in ways that will develop creative and innovative problem-solving skills. You don't learn how to tackle problems and seek out ways to achieve success. When you are faced with difficulties, they may seem overwhelming, and you may not even try to find ways to solve the problem.

Self-Efficacy Variability

Whether you have a generally positive or negative self-efficacy belief, your belief in yourself and your capabilities will vary depending on the task or type of task you are facing. The same previously mentioned influences that affect self-belief in general impact the variability of your self-efficacy depending on the task at hand.

For example, if you have failed at a task before, you are less likely to believe that you can succeed at the same task or similar tasks in the future. However, if you have experienced success in the past, you are more likely to face the same or similar tasks with positive self-efficacy in the future.

Both positive and negative self-efficacy exist in every individual. Just because you have positive self-efficacy in some aspects of life doesn't mean you won't have poor self-efficacy in others. In part, this is what makes self-efficacy such a complex part of who you are and of what you believe yourself to be capable.

Developing and having positive self-belief is vital to achieving personal success in life. It helps you overcome your fears and move past negative experiences. One of the greatest determinants of success is believing in yourself.

Your self-esteem can very well take a knock if you experience failure in one area of life, but it's up to you to pick yourself up, dust yourself off, and keep trying. Our failures serve as a learning curve and an indication of the right direction to head in.

"Failure is success in progress."

— ALBERT EINSTEIN

What Einstein was saying is that making mistakes and occasionally failing should help develop strong positive self-efficacy. You keep trying, and therefore, you become a champion in whatever it is you are trying to achieve.

My personal experience: Practical exams called OSCEs were required while working toward my Nursing Degree. I had a lot of experience in carrying out patient clinical observations (Early Warning Score) thanks to previously working as a healthcare assistant. Having this experience, I didn't bother to practice the necessary tasks involved in patient observations. I believed I knew everything I needed to know to pass my OSCEs with flying colors.

Despite performing well in other OSCEs, I was evaluated in taking manual blood pressure. I failed this exam because I was only familiar with taking blood pressure electronically with vital signs monitors. Failing the exam came as a profound shock to my system. After all, I had experience in patient observation. All my friends all passed, and yet they had no previous real-life experience.

My self-efficacy took a big knock in this aspect, and although I was given another opportunity to take blood pressure manually, I failed the exam again. I made mistakes throughout the evaluation, and I was so nervous I was literally shaking. This second failure occurred because my self-esteem had taken a blow in the previous exam and my self-belief was low.

To help myself overcome my poor self-efficacy in taking manual blood pressure, I had to focus on my past successes. I had to remind myself of the real-life experience I had, of the other written exams I had passed, and my good performances in previous placements. I had to remind myself of the goal I was trying to achieve. I had to think logically and realize that a single failed exam was not the end of the world and should not prevent me from reaching that goal.

Having considered and acknowledged these things, I was determined to pass the exam. My determination to pass the course, my self-perception, and my personal motivation in order to complete my goal allowed me to practice hard for positive results. The third time's the charm, as they say, and I passed the third exam. After that, I became excellent at taking manual blood pressure. Many nurses shy away from using the manual method because it is more complicated than taking blood pressure with the help of electronic monitors, yet manual blood pressure is believed to be more accurate.

The moral of my personal experience is this: Failure is part of the path toward success. Don't let failure prevent you from working toward your goal. Take accountability for your actions and use failure to improve your self-efficacy.

SOURCES OF SELF-BELIEF

Positive or negative self-efficacy isn't something you are simply born with. It is something you learn, and during that learning process, there are a variety of things that may influence how your self-efficacy develops.

Experience

The strongest influence on perceived self-efficacy is experience. Your experiences in life, both successes and failures, shape whether you believe yourself capable or incapable. Succeeding at tasks builds a strong positive self-belief. Failing builds a negative self-belief. Failures are especially influential in undermining your belief in yourself if they occur before your overall self-belief is fully developed.

Even though success can foster a positive belief in yourself, you could easily be discouraged when you do fail if those successes come too easily. When success is hard-earned through persistence and overcoming the obstacles between you and your goal, a resilient positive self-belief is created.

Everybody wants success to come easily but hard-won successes are actually good for you. They make you stronger and more resilient in the face of life's difficulties. When you have to work to succeed, you learn to continually put in the effort, keep at it, and quickly get up and dust yourself off when setbacks happen.

According to Dr. Joe Dispenza, author of Breaking the Habit of Being Yourself: How to Lose Your Mind and Create a New One, your thoughts become habitual. Your thoughts about your self-efficacy become automatic, even subconscious. Once those thought patterns are established, you may not even realize you are thinking negatively about your self-efficacy because it just comes naturally after a while. For this reason, it is vital to monitor how you think and feel about yourself to determine negative self-efficacy perceptions in order to challenge and change them.

"If you think about it, people wake up in the morning, they begin to think about their problems, those problems are circuits, memories in the brain. Each one of those memories is connected to people and things at certain times and places and if the brain is a record of

the past, the moment they start their day they're already thinking in the past."

— (TEAMSOUL, 2018)

What does this mean in terms of perceived self-efficacy? Your past experiences create habitual thoughts that become a self-fulfilling prophecy for future ventures. You are essentially living in the past.

We know that we cannot change our past, but we can work on our present. If your past negatively affects your current self-efficacy, it is your responsibility, as a compos mentis person, to control your thoughts, your plans, and your actions. Use your past as a learning experience. It is up to you to learn from your failures, tortures, pain, or achievements. When your mind dwells on an experience from your past; use it to facilitate your future. Train your brain to use your experience to better your present and your future. Eventually, you will be able to do this naturally and without thought, like breathing. The key to successfully retraining your brain to do what you want it to do and not hold you back is consistency. You must be consistent in changing how your mind interprets and relates to past experiences.

My personal experience: My mother encouraged me to do well at mathematics when I entered secondary school because of how important the subject was and because I struggled so much with it in primary school. When I completed primary school, my older sister spent time teaching me numeracy to help me master math. Upon entering secondary school, bursaries were offered to students who excelled at math. I put in an incredible amount of effort to study hard and stand out head-and-shoulders above the rest to earn those bursaries. My hard work paid off, and I earned bursary after bursary for excelling at my studies.

Everybody believed I was just naturally very clever, but I knew differently. I knew it was due to all the hard work I put into studying that allowed me to excel and earn the bursaries. I believed in myself. My strong belief in my ability to study hard and do well lead me to put in the effort required to perform well according to the academic standards set out by the school.

In this example of my own experience, my perceived self-efficacy was the belief that I had the ability to study hard and be the best, earning bursaries along the way. It did not mean that I was necessarily capable of being the best. It just meant that I believed strongly that I was able to do so.

At the time, a friend of mine was not doing well at all. In fact, they never even tried to do well. My friend, like others, believed that I was simply clever and had a natural knack to excel. She also believed that she was not clever. She even believed she was so academically poor that she could not understand her own handwriting at times. My friend had the belief that there was no point in trying or putting any effort into her studies because she was wholly convinced, she was not capable of doing well. That belief in her inability to do well was her negative perceived self-efficacy and it dictated her actions toward the task; it led her to give up trying.

As you can see from my childhood story, personal experiences have a big role to play in how you perceive your own self-efficacy. I had a history of struggling in mathematics in primary school. I hated it so much, which was another reason I chose to work hard at becoming better at it in secondary school. I believed I could do well irrespective of capability and put in the hard work which ultimately paid off. My friend, on the other hand, got stuck in her past. Her negative experience developed a poor perception of herself. It is up to you to use your past as a reason to work hard to change your here and now and your future just like I did.

Social Persuasion

Social persuasion is how the opinions and beliefs of others about you affect your perceived self-efficacy. If others tell you that you are capable of success, you are more likely to persevere and put more effort into what you need to do to achieve success. If others tell you that you are not capable of success, chances are you will not even try. If you do try, you aren't likely to put in much effort, and the more difficulty you experience in your efforts, the less likely you are to keep at it.

There is a potential problem with social persuasion in developing positive beliefs in your ability to achieve success. It's easier for the discouragement by others to undermine your self-belief than it is for positive encouragement in your capabilities to build it up. Why? You will quickly stop believing in the encouragement from others if you are disappointed with the outcome of your efforts to succeed despite having received a self-belief boost from social persuasion.

If you are discouraged, you develop a tendency to give up easily or avoid potential challenges altogether. In this way, your poor self-belief actually creates a repetitive cycle by negatively influencing your efforts. If you believe you will fail, you will not put in the effort needed to succeed or persevere when setbacks happen, and inevitably, you won't succeed.

My personal experience: Part of my belief in myself came from the support of my family.

I didn't always excel academically. During my primary school years, I actually struggled with my studies, but my mother didn't let my struggles deter me. She believed in me, and she believed in my self-efficacy. My family believed so strongly in my ability to do better that my sister got involved, tutoring me in numeracy. This social persuasion created a more positive perceived self-efficacy and provided me with a good experience that encouraged me to put in hard work. When that hard work paid off and I did excel, the experience bolstered my self-efficacy, causing me to believe in myself and give it my all when taking on future tasks.

Remember my friend who wasn't doing well and didn't even want to try because of her poor perceived self-efficacy? She had a completely different experience of social persuasion from mine. Unlike my mother, who believed in me and taught me to believe in myself, her mother was the opposite. She confided in me that her mother didn't believe she could do better either. This combination of experiencing failure and being told by others that she could not do better created negatively perceived self-efficacy. If my mother did not believe in me and didn't encourage me, I may never have believed in myself, which may have led to me not even trying.

How we treat others can make or break their self-efficacy beliefs. When we discourage them, they develop poor self-efficacy. Believing in and encouraging those you care about can have a dramatic impact on their lives and their beliefs about the world, their place in it, and themselves. Think about this: what experience are you providing your loved ones that could contribute to shaping their perceived self-efficacy?

Ask yourself these two very important questions:

1. *"What do people around me say about me?"*
2. *"How do the people around me influence my perceived self-efficacy?"*

The answers to these two questions are vitally important for how you perceive yourself. There will be two camps. You will have positive, encouraging believers. You will also have negative, discouraging disbelievers. If you find that the disbelievers have a profound influence on your perceived self-efficacy, it may be time to either cut ties, limit what you share with them, or confront them about their negativity towards you.

Over time, being surrounded by people who do not believe in you can cause you to develop negative self-efficacy. Think about it this way: if people persuade you to doubt yourself, you are likely to have poor self-belief. Poor self-belief often breeds general negativity about life, and you may end up seeking out other similarly negative people, perpetuating a negative cycle.

My personal experience: I was once told by a friend that I would never be rich. This had a profound impact on me because their disbelief in my abilities and what they said constantly played on my mind. What helped me through this situation was my pre-existing positive self-belief. My positive self-efficacy was developed through experience and the positive beliefs of my mother. I had been so strongly encouraged, worked so hard, and came so far. I wasn't about to let one unfounded comment completely discourage and destroy me.

I confronted the friend who had made the unkind comment and I did so from a position of love and understanding. I shared the fact that I had managed to achieve 80 percent of my dream, and because of my achievements I believed I was already prosperous. I reminded my friend that what wealth means to one person may mean something different to another. In life, we are all pursuing the same goal: to be our truest selves. This can vary from person to person.

Social persuasion can be a powerful determining factor in your perception of yourself if you allow it to be. Sometimes, you need to learn to take what others think or say about you with a 'pinch of salt' or let it go altogether. Her belief in me may be based on her own beliefs about herself and the world at large. It may not actually be about me at all. Confronting my friend about her negativity helped me address her negative beliefs that created her poor perception of me. Her perception was based on the belief that unless you invested in her kind of trading, you cannot be prosperous and successful. That was relevant to her own beliefs but not to mine.

Important note: When confronting others about their negative perception of you, it is important to approach them from a compassionate and mindful position instead of a defensive or hostile angle. You need to have healthy self-efficacy before confronting negativity or you may risk further damaging your self-belief. You could end up walking away with negativity, bitterness, anger, or even lower self-esteem than before.

Social Modeling

Social modeling believes you can do something by being influenced by the success of people around you or those you look up to. When you see people, who are similar to you succeed in what they set out to do through hard work and perseverance, you develop the belief that you can also succeed if you put in the same effort and perseverance. You believe that you have the same capabilities they do.

Social modeling can also have the opposite effect of negatively influencing your self-efficacy. If you see people with similar capabilities, put in the hard work and persevere with their efforts and fail at a task, you are more likely to develop the belief that you can't succeed at related tasks. Another potential negative effect is viewing someone as similar to yourself when they are, in fact, quite different. Perceiving someone as similar and using them as a self-efficacy role model could be harmful when you see them succeed, but you don't. Sometimes it's easy to overlook the possible differences, which could contribute to the difference in performance.

Society can have a strong influence on how you view yourself and your self-belief, and it can be easy to lose yourself in the beliefs and limitations of the society you live in. Society has the tendency to encourage comparisons between your own success and that of others as opposed to appreciating each person's individuality. It is vitally important to acknowledge and remember that each individual is unique and has their own unique gifts.

You may have experiences or skills similar to those of someone else, but the fact that you are unique and not a carbon copy of anyone else creates differences in experiences and abilities. Understanding that you are unique and possess your own set of gifts is liberating. It minimizes comparing yourself to others, which will help improve your self-esteem. Identifying your special gifts is something you need to do right now, not later. It is the source of your personal strength and power.

Once you have identified your gifts, your job is to align your personality with those gifts, which will bring you a sense of fulfillment by helping you find your purpose in life. Understanding what makes you unique and discovering your purpose increases your confidence and self-efficacy. You are then able to emancipate yourself from the negative influence societal beliefs and expectations can have on you through social modeling. Being confident in your abilities does not mean that you see yourself as better than others; it simply means you understand that you are different and unique. You will no longer use others as a self-efficacy role model and benchmark for success. You will realize that you do not control them or their actions — you only control your own beliefs and the action you take toward improving yourself.

If you realize that your self-efficacy is being negatively influenced by the community around you, a move to a different community may be an option. In some cases, it can be beneficial to move to another area, make different friends, or spend less time with people who exert a negative influence over you. In some instances, you can even help others change if that is something you can do. The important thing to remember is that you must not give up simply because someone else has failed or given up. Your goal is to create a fulfilling life by helping yourself discover your individuality and realizing that you have the ability to do it.

Ask yourself this very important question: Do you know what your special gifts are that make you unique? If the answer is 'no,' it's time to start working on discovering your unique gifts. If the answer is 'yes,' it's time to align your skills and personality with that gift if you haven't already done so.

Social modeling isn't all bad, though. It can provide you with a social role model who possesses the abilities you are trying to build up. A good social role model is able to pass on knowledge and skills to their observers, ultimately building up the self-efficacy of those observers.

According to Buunk and Gibbons (2007) and Van Lange (2008), the concept we have of ourselves, and our self-esteem is greatly influenced by social comparisons we make between ourselves and others. Comparisons are made based on beliefs, behavior, and attitude relative to those of others. Through social comparison, we learn about our skills, our capabilities, the validity of our opinions, and our place in society.

Social comparison is not limited to real people around us; we often compare ourselves to fictional characters, such as those in stories and on TV. We make these comparisons between ourselves and others we view as important. However, the strongest sources of social comparisons are people we perceive as similar to us.

Most social comparisons involve aspects of life that don't have a basis in hard facts but rather are determined according to the opinions and beliefs of other people. Deciding what to wear for an occasion or even in daily life is a good example. We also base our skills, aptitudes, and capabilities on our comparisons to others. An example of such a comparison is a student using a class average to determine how well they performed. If they performed better than the average, their self-efficacy is positively influenced. If their result was below the average, poor self-efficacy can develop because of comparing their performance to that of their peers.

There are two types of social comparison: downward and upward comparison. Upward comparison is when we compare ourselves to others whom we perceive as better or who perform better. This can have a negative impact on self-esteem because we often feel bad when we are either not equal to or do worse than others. However, the upward social comparison is not necessarily harmful. If we use it as a positive influence, it can provide us with inspiration and modeling for improving our performance and achieving our goals.

Downward social comparison is when we compare ourselves to those who are doing worse than us. Our self-esteem receives a boost, and we feel better about ourselves, which helps develop positive self-efficacy.

Mental and Physical Well Being

Your mood and how you feel physically play a pivotal role in regard to your perceived self-efficacy, as well as your level of motivation. If you are experiencing a blue mood or feel physically unwell, you are likely to feel incapable of successfully completing a task or facing a challenge. It also works the other way around. If you are in a good mood and feel physically well, chances are you will experience improved self-belief and resilience if setbacks or obstacles do crop up.

The effect of low self-esteem on social relationships:

Self-esteem plays a role in the success and health of your social interaction. When your self-esteem is low, you feel bad about yourself; you feel as though you aren't good enough, and eventually, your relationships suffer. You may avoid social activities altogether, reducing your ability and likelihood of making new connections and deteriorating your existing interpersonal relationships.

The effect of low self-esteem on stress: When faced with something stressful, you have two thought processes. You first evaluate how stressful something is going to be, and then you evaluate your ability to cope with that stress and overcome it. Your self-esteem affects your perception of and ability to cope with stressors. Having low-self-esteem may cause you to believe that you don't have the ability and resources to cope with stress. Believing that you are not able to cope with stress may lead to experiencing situations more stressfully and with more anxiety.

Low self-esteem and mental health: having low self-esteem is not a mental health problem in itself, but it can lead to the development of or increase in severity of mental health issues. Experiencing low self-esteem for a prolonged period of time may increase anxiety and contribute to the development of mental illnesses, such as depression. On the flip side, having an existing mental health condition may lead to developing poor self-esteem. Suffering from a mental health condition, such as depression, whether it existed before and led to low self-esteem or if low self-esteem led to its development, can leave you feeling helpless and unable to cope or make changes to improve your perception of yourself.

Media

What you see in magazines, on social media, and on television may well dictate what you believe about yourself. Self-efficacy is not just about talents or performing tasks. It can encompass everything about you, from the way you look, to what behavior is and is not acceptable, to what qualities are valued or not.

The media generally purports an image of extremes. On the one side, there are beautiful, capable, idealized characters or people. On the other side, there are unattractive, incapable, and undervalued people or characters. The idealized people and characters the media love to bombard you with are attractive, desirable, and strong-willed, with the ability to overcome unrealistically insurmountable odds. The rest are relegated to villains, the ugly friends, the unloved ones, background extras, and more.

This disparity between the people and characters that are either idolized or outcast affects your self-efficacy due to how you relate to them. If you find you relate easily to a person or character that is undervalued or shunned, you are likely to find yourself stuck in the same mindset they have: a mindset of not being able to achieve your dreams and goals. Finding the idealized characters or people more relatable boosts your sense of self-efficacy. Why? You are identifying with the go-getters, the achievers, the characters everybody puts on a pedestal.

Following the media undoubtedly has its benefits, but it's not all sunshine and roses. Your perception of yourself can be positively influenced, but it can also be negatively affected to your detriment. It can have such a negative impact that it sabotages your mental health. Any one of a number of things put out by media platforms can influence your perception of yourself. Many culprits of negative social influence are unrealistic images, catchphrases, or stories. We will often compare ourselves to the characters in the stories we read, the images we see, or edgy slogans we hear.

Comparing yourself to anything that is unrealistic creates a negative perception of yourself. You may end up picking yourself apart because you cannot live up to the expectations you place on yourself because of the unrealistic and skewed perception media stimuli can create. Almost everything on social media is not real. It is staged, or it's Photoshopped, or its reality has been altered in some other way. It can tear your self-efficacy apart and leave you feeling dissatisfied with who you are.

When real people put things out onto social media, they are showing you what they want you to see, not necessarily what is real. Social media can make you believe that it's real, but you don't know what the person behind the picture is thinking, feeling, or going through. A smiling picture may be hiding great pain and dissatisfaction. You cannot tell the truth about what is going on in their hearts, minds, or lives without being in their shoes. Comparing yourself to these people or believing everything on social media will only lower your self-efficacy and hold you back from moving forward.

My personal experience: An example of the influence of social media on self-efficacy is a vivid memory I have of a past experience. I was off sick from work and at home in my bed. I ventured onto Facebook and posted a lovely picture of myself sitting in a swing chair in a friend's garden. I captioned the picture with, 'Now it's Monday. Hope you have either gone out and made some money or stayed in and added some value to yourself. Self-care is self-love.'

The picture I posted had been taken roughly a month before I posted it on Facebook. The only reason I used that particular picture is that it was the first picture I came across. After about two hours, I began receiving text messages. The messages were all asking me how I do it, who did my garden, and some of my friends asking when they could pop round to visit me.

This is a prime example of people posting on social media what they want others to see instead of posting what is real. It certainly was an eye-opener for me, and my experience should be an eye-opener for you. Think about what you see on social media platforms, and don't always take everything at face value. There's a better than good chance it's not real or not the whole truth being put out there.

If this all sounds like doom and gloom for social media, do not worry. It is possible to develop a healthy relationship with social media. In fact, it is imperative to your self-efficacy and wellbeing that you do everything you can to maintain a healthy perception of social media. There are several ways in which you can maintain the balance between social media life and real life. These methods will help keep you sane and believing in yourself while preventing you from falling into the trap of comparison between reality and unrealistic ideas of perfection.

Stay focused on yourself: If you allow yourself to get sucked into a virtual world, you can lose perspective about yourself and life in general. This loss of perspective can disconnect you from who you are in reality and lead to a deterioration in your perceived self-efficacy through constant comparisons. Maintain a healthy perspective by keeping the focus on your true self and your real life without making those comparisons.

See the real you: Much of what is in the media is edited or one-sided. You don't get to see the other side of the story or the unedited images. This creates a false sense of what is and what should be. Basing your self-efficacy and judgment of what you should be capable of or achieve on content that is not real or only one-sided is unhelpful. It is important to remain grounded in your own reality and keep perspective of who you are and what you are capable of instead of living in a virtual world that can encourage you to feel like a failure when you aren't.

Limit your social media time: Part of getting sucked into social media and the unrealistic world within it is spending too much time on social media platforms. You end up losing not only perspective but also precious time you could be using to reach your goals in life instead of running yourself down with comparisons. Focus more of your time on yourself and less on social media. Limiting social media time can be difficult and the temptation to 'just take a quick look' is often high with mobile apps at your fingertips all the time. If you are having difficulty resisting that temptation and scaling back how much time you spend on social media, try uninstalling those apps.

Understand that comparisons are not helpful: The media, including the internet, social media, and magazines, are filled with images and stories of what society deems to be praise-worthy or perfect. It is important to understand that comparing yourself to someone else in any way, shape, or form can be unhelpful and even unhealthy. Taking inspiration from a story or image is one thing. Directly comparing yourself to it is another and won't help you work toward reaching your own goals in life.

Avoid triggers: There may be images, ideas, slogans, or lifestyles that trigger your unhealthy comparisons and self-doubt, which lower your sense of self-efficacy. Identify these media stimuli and avoid them when and where possible. The simplest way to do this is to unfollow potentially triggering social media accounts. However, social media and the internet, in general, are very clever. Your search history may be tracked and recorded, which can still keep triggering content cropping up as you scroll through social media. Clean out all browsing history across all devices. It's like starting with a clean slate and no search history to prompt triggering content advertisements and suggestions.

Sometimes triggers may come from people close to you who might post things seemingly aimed at you personally. Sometimes you may not be the target, but if you feel disturbed by certain posts to the extent that your self-esteem is being affected, then you need to do something about it. When triggers come from your close relations, it can be difficult to deal with the problem, but it's not impossible. You don't have to make the drastic decision to unfriend them; all you have to do is unfollow them or block their posts from appearing on your newsfeed. The effects of unfollowing someone vary from one social media platform to another, but generally, it will prevent you from seeing that person's posts or getting notifications. This can help prevent friction within relationships, as the person being unfollowed won't be notified and there will be no unpleasant fallout.

Live your dream, do not just wish it through social media: While social media can be an external influence on your perception of yourself, it can also be an internal source of personal turmoil. Just like others can present the world with an idealized image of themselves on social media, do not fall in that trap too. Avoid spending all your time trying to present yourself and your life to the world in the way you want to be seen instead of actually living your dream. In this sense, social media is a form of escapism that prevents you from dealing with the problems and issues that will impede your ability to achieve your goal.

Hold yourself accountable: You are responsible for your own success in life. Living your life on social media stands in your way of working toward your dreams and goals. It is time to take responsibility for your actions and hold yourself accountable for how much time you spend on social media, how much you allow it to influence you, and how much it distracts you from real life.

There is nothing wrong with taking a timeout from social media by deciding to abstain from it for a period of time, like a week or so. You can concentrate on working toward your goals during this time. You may be surprised by just how much time you can channel into making progress toward personal achievements by taking a social media timeout once a month. You control your social media — it doesn't control you.

Culture

Culture can play a big role in your perceived self-efficacy. Across cultures, many people experience self-enhancement bias. You tend to highlight your own good qualities or attributes in comparison to others. However, how much you do to enhance those good qualities may come down to your culture. It's suggested that cultures that place priority on the collective, or their society as a whole, are less likely to praise an individual's achievements, and individuals are less likely to be competitive and seek validation. This results in fewer individuals from that culture being inclined to actively enhance themselves. The contrary is true of cultures that place value on individualism, encourage competition, and praise achievement. Individuals in these cultures are more likely to put a lot of effort into self-enhancement.

How does this affect self-efficacy? Cultures that emphasize the community as a whole over individual achievement may foster a lower sense of self-efficacy because standing out isn't encouraged. On the other hand, coming from a culture that praises individualism and personal achievement may nurture a better sense of self-efficacy because putting the effort and persistence into reaching personal goals is encouraged.

Transitioning from one culture to another poses a problem for many migrants. The majority of these migrants suffer from low self-efficacy. According to the United Nations, there were 272 million migrants across the world by 2019, accounting for 3.5% of the global population (International Organization for Migration, 2019). Migrating from a culture that believes in and supports achieving communal goals to one that promotes and supports pursuing and achieving individual goals poses a potential problem. Migrants making this move tend to suffer from poor self-efficacy because they have an ingrained belief to achieve communal goals.

Standing out and achieving personal goals to such migrants is a foreign concept for them. They may not be accustomed to speaking their mind and explaining themselves. The outcome may be aggressive rather than assertive as a defense mechanism for their poor self-efficacy beliefs for achieving personal goals.

The new culture they may be living in may have different expectations from the society they came from. The affected migrants may need to embrace the new concepts. The willingness to change their beliefs and responsivities is crucial to fitting in and adopting a new societal culture. Just because immigrants may have always worked towards collective success doesn't mean they don't have the inner strength or the ability to achieve individual success. They just have to tap into that strength and develop positive self-efficacy and their desire for personal success.

Gender

Men and women may experience differences in self-efficacy. This comes down to societal conditioning regarding what the norms are and gender roles within a culture or society. A typical example would be that women are not generally considered to have a place in a workshop as a mechanic, while men are supposed to be technical and skilled with their hands. This could lead to a generalized perception of self-efficacy wherein women may not believe that they can perform technical tasks, such as with automobile maintenance or carpentry. On the other hand, men may have a better perception of their self-efficacy for technical tasks because it's a normal societal perception that men should be good at such activities.

Studies conducted in the United States between 1946 and 2018 have shown great shifts in the roles men and women play in modern life. These studies showed that women have stepped further and further into roles and areas of life that were previously male dominated while the presence of men in these areas has decreased.

In 1950, the presence of women in the labor force was 32%. This rose to 57% in 2018. On the other side of the equation, men's participation in the labor force fell from 82% in 1950 to 69% in 2018. (U.S. Bureau of Labor Statistics, 2017, 2018b).

On an educational front, according to Okahana and Zhou (2018), women's education levels have risen considerably. Women are now earning more bachelor's, master's, and doctoral degrees than their male counterparts.

These studies prove that gender roles are changing, and socially held concepts of gender stereotypes should, too. In fact, they are slowly changing, as both men and women diversify their roles and gender equality increases. These studies also highlight the importance of recognizing these changes in gender role perceptions as a steppingstone to building positive self-efficacy.

Cross-cultural influences are helping change cultural ideals that are not applicable in a gender-equal world. This migration from one cultural society to the next helps provide exposure to people with previously set or limited ideas about gender roles. It can be seen as a cross-cultural pollination of more positive and unrestricted beliefs about societal norms.

Whether you are a woman stepping into a previously male-dominated role or a man stepping into a role previously only relegated to the 'fairer sex,' believing in yourself is the key to your success. Allowing society to dictate who you should be, what you should want, and what you can achieve based on outdated gender stereotypes is not going to get you anywhere.

You need to learn to break free from limiting beliefs, such as traditional gender roles. Believing in yourself is personal; it is part of your personality, and therefore it goes with you everywhere and influences every aspect of your life. Basing your self-belief on societal expectations limits what you think you are capable of. In turn, poor self-belief limits the effort you will put into reaching a goal that is outside societal norms, decreasing your chances of achieving that goal. Knowing what you want in life and believing in yourself is the first step to making your dream a reality.

My personal experience: My husband and I don't abide by societal ideas of gender norms. Regardless of what society says is the woman's job, whichever one of us gets home first takes on the tasks of cooking a meal and looking after our children. Much to my surprise, he has actually gained fantastic cooking skills and prepares delicious meals! However, within his own culture, it's not at all common for men to do the cooking. Having migrated to a different cultural society has brought a newfound open-mindedness to his outlook and beliefs. My husband has positive self-efficacy beliefs. He strongly believes that he can do anything he wants to do and puts his mind to and not just what his culture dictates he can. This change in beliefs and positive self-efficacy has allowed us to live a very fulfilling family life.

Sometimes it comes down to ignoring traditional cultural beliefs that limit the expectations of what you are capable of or what you should be capable of. It allows you to raise the bar and improve your self-belief, which goes hand-in-hand with achieving your personal goals.

When you base your self-efficacy on what your culture or the society you live in believes as a collective, you are putting your happiness and your relationships at risk. Limiting yourself for the sake of cultural or societal approval may be the root of your unhappiness and failed relationships. Even if you share a similar culture or live in a similar society as your partner, your relationship is personal and unique, and it will place demands on both of you that are unique to your relationship with each other. You need to embrace your own self-belief irrespective of what others say in order to nurture your relationships.

Familial Sources of Self-Efficacy

The origins of your perceived self-efficacy can be traced back to your formative years as a child. From birth to the age of about eight years old, you undergo intense and rapid development. This is the time in your life when you expand your cognitive, emotional, language, social, and physical capabilities. During your development in these areas, you learn about yourself and begin to develop self-efficacy.

Throughout all of this development, you are testing your capabilities, and with each test of your ability, you are also evaluating how effective you are at it. A good example of an area of development where self-efficacy is constantly tested and evaluated is the development and expansion of your sensorimotor skills. Learning these skills allows you to explore more of the world around you and provides you with a greater opportunity to respond to it.

This is where parental interaction comes in to help develop positive self-efficacy. Parents have the power to mold a child's sense of self-efficacy through how they respond to their children. Another way in which parents influence the development of self-efficacy is by providing their children with opportunities to face and overcome challenges. It is important, though, that parents do not set the bar too high and provide opportunities to face challenges that are appropriate for a child's age and skill level. Positive responses to achieving tasks and acquiring skills help build positive self-efficacy. Facing challenges that require effort to overcome but are still within a child's scope of capability provides a personal sense of achievement and boosts self-esteem.

Families also play a role in the development of negative self-efficacy in children. A lack of positive response and encouragement from parents may leave a child feeling as though they have not achieved enough, even if they have had success. Children may also compare themselves to their siblings, with younger siblings potentially falling victim to comparing themselves with older, more advanced, and capable siblings.

When a child makes these comparisons between themselves and their siblings, it is important for parents to acknowledge and teach them that they are unique, special, and have their own unique gifts. Positive responses to personal achievements will further enhance positive self-efficacy and minimize the desire to make comparisons.

3

THE PROCESS OF SELF-CONCILIATION

In this chapter, we will cover the topic of self-conciliation. That is a pretty big, fancy word right there. Before we delve deeper into the components of self-conciliation, perhaps we should clear up what it means.

WHAT IS SELF-CONCILIATION?

Our initial reaction to words that seem big, or confusing is, 'What on earth does that even mean? What are you talking about?' Breaking a word down into its individual pieces can be helpful in understanding what it means. In the case of self-conciliation, there are two parts: self and conciliation.

Self is pretty explanatory. It means you or yourself; it has to do with something you are doing yourself without external assistance or without going to an external source for help. A good example is self-help. The word 'self' is used to indicate that you are helping yourself without getting someone to help you.

Conciliation is a bit trickier. Most of us know the word reconciliation. In the case of self-conciliation, the 're' has been taken away and only 'conciliation' used. The definition of conciliation is:

"The action of bringing peace and harmony; the action of ending strife."

— (YOURDICTIONARY.COM)

Self-conciliation, therefore, means reconciling with yourself. You are going through the process of making peace with yourself to bring harmony to your inner workings and end the conflict and difficulties you experience within yourself.

Now that we have a better understanding of what self-conciliation means, let us take a closer look at how you go about doing it and what the benefits are.

THE SELF-CONSTRUAL THEORY

Here we go again, another big, confusing word. Self-construal has to do with how you define yourself independently as well as based on cultural influences. It's your understanding of who you are in relation to the society and culture you live in. Self-construal can also be seen as your self-image.

There are two main types of self-construal: independent and interdependent. Independent self-construal refers to how you view yourself independently from others. Interdependent self-construal refers to how you view yourself in relation to others. It is possible to have both types of self-construal, but one is likely to be more dominant. Let's take a closer look at each of these self-construal and their influence.

Independent Self-Construal

Independent self-construal has to do with defining yourself independently from others and society as a whole. How you define yourself is mostly based on your own thoughts, skills, capabilities, and attitude. How you view yourself does not depend on your relationships with others or how others perceive you. You are likely to view yourself as unique and focus on what sets you apart from others as opposed to what makes you similar.

Interdependent Self-Construal

Interdependent self-construal has to do with feeling strongly and deeply connected to others. Your focus is not on yourself, but on your community. You are more likely to align yourself with ways you can enhance society or your social group. You identify your self-image by your connections with others and the role you play socially.

Determining Self-Construal

There is one simple question you can ask yourself to help you determine which type of self-construal is dominant within you.

'Who am I?'

If independent self-construal is more dominant, you are likely to answer that question with personal qualities that set you apart as a unique individual. You may provide answers like 'I am confident' or 'I am creative.' These answers highlight the emphasis you put on yourself as being distinct from everyone else.

If interdependent self-construal is more dominant, you are likely to answer that question with references to who you are in terms of social connections and relationships. You may provide answers like 'I am a sister' or 'I am part of a book club.' These answers highlight the emphasis you put on defining yourself by your role in a relationship or group.

In life, the sooner you ask yourself this question and provide yourself with an answer, the quicker you can align yourself with the things that will help you advance toward your goals and dreams. This includes aligning yourself with:

- The right people.
- The right education.
- The right career.

It's a pity that our hormones run so rampant during our teenage years that there is little thought or consideration given to such an important question. Yet, it would be incredibly beneficial to present teenagers with this question and have them answer it. Discovering the answer to this question could help steer young individuals in the right direction for achieving their goals and prevent them from getting distracted from their dreams.

While it's always better to start sooner and younger, it's never too late to discover who you are and how to achieve your goals. Irrespective of your age or where you are in your life, you have the ability to make a fresh start because life is what you make it.

Finding out exactly who you are is one of the most important discoveries you will ever make in your life. If you are not happy with the answers you provide to that question, the next question to ask yourself is:

'Who do I want to be?'

This is a crucial fundamental question that will help you figure out who you really want to be, and then work toward becoming that person by properly aligning your thoughts, actions, beliefs, and values with that dream.

In order to be who you want to be, do you have to:

- Get further education?
- Teach people about things that are important to you?
- Change friendships or make new ones?
- Work on relationships?
- Relocate to a new city or even a new country?
- Be more helpful to your community or humanity in general?
- Write a book?
- Start a family or grow your existing family?

Whatever it is that will help you become the person you really want to be, take that leap of faith and make it happen. Life is too short to postpone self-development, and you only get to live once. Can you imagine anything worse than coming to the end of your life and only being able to think about the person you wanted to be, but never took action to help yourself become that person? Keep this in mind: you are a compos mentis adult, and you have the power to change the world you live in. Believing in yourself, being true to yourself, and developing healthy positive self-efficacy is vital to living a fulfilled life.

Culture and Self-Construal

Culture has a strong influence on how you view and define yourself. Your self-construal may be largely shaped by the type of culture you live in. If you live in a collectivist culture where priority is placed on the community rather than the individual, you are likely to have dominant independent self-construal. People living in an individualistic culture where priority is placed on the individual over the community are likely to have dominant independent self-construal.

However, that's not to say that living in a collectivist culture automatically causes high dominance in interdependent self-construal. People have varying levels of both self-construals. All it means is that culture exerts a strong influence over whether you are likely to develop a higher independent or interdependent self-construal. Your self-construal may also be primed or manipulated to adapt to the culture you live in by changing the way you think about and view yourself.

The Influence of Self-Construal

Self-construal influences three main areas of your life: interpersonal relationships, social interaction, and self-esteem. Individuals with interdependent and independent self-construal approach interpersonal relationships differently and interact with others differently. This demonstrates a correlation between self-construal type and self-esteem.

Self-Construal and Self-Esteem

Self-construal affects how you view and behave toward others, but it also plays an integral role in how you view and feel about yourself. It's suggested that:

- Individuals living in an individualistic culture and having a higher independent self-construal tend to have higher self-esteem.
- Individuals living in a collectivist culture and having a higher interdependent self-construal tend to have lower self-esteem.

— (HEINE ET AL. 1999)

This research shows a correlation between your dominant self-construal and your self-esteem. Independent self-construal usually comes with the desire to advance yourself and therefore your thoughts and actions will be self-serving. A dominant interdependent self-construal usually comes with the desire to please and benefit the group or community, which inherently brings about thoughts and actions that are selfless or less self-serving.

In short, having more independent self-construal is associated with having healthier self-views and more positive self-efficacy.

Understanding your self-construal will allow you to make informed decisions about your goals. It can become easier to decide where you want to invest or focus your career when you realize who you are in relation to the culture or society you live in. You may want to avoid careers that focus on teamwork or serving others if you have dominant independent self-construal. If you have dominant interdependent self-construal, a team environment or a job that serves others is the way to go. You will find fulfillment and satisfaction when your job aligns with your self-construal.

Self-Construal and Interpersonal Relationships

Your self-identity, or self-construal, is intimately linked to how you approach and handle interpersonal relationships of all kinds and how you interact with others. These relationships are important to both types of self-construal for different reasons.

For those with dominant interdependent self-construal, interpersonal relationships are incredibly important because of the inclination to define oneself according to your connections with others. Your self-identity emphasizes being part of a group over being distinctly individual and unique. You are more likely to want to please and benefit others within your social group, even potentially to your own detriment.

Your desire to identify with a group is such that you may even manage your emotional responses and change your behavior toward others to maintain harmonious interaction. In fact, your emotional responses will differ from those of individuals with dominant independent self-construal. You are inclined to experience emotions known as 'other-focused.' These emotional responses focus on how others are feeling instead of focusing on what you are feeling. You are also more inclined to listen to the other person and see things from their perspective, thus altering the way you perceive yourself and the world around you.

While this may be a good thing, it does have its downsides. You may be more empathetic toward others, but you may also be less likely to stand your ground if you don't agree with someone else. For example, take a situation where you are doing something that is not strictly wrong, but someone checks you on your behavior because they don't appreciate it. You are more likely to take on their perspective, emphasize their feelings over your own, and feel ashamed of that behavior. You may even possibly alter your behavior going forward to avoid possible future conflict and maintain relationship harmony.

Viewing your interpersonal relationships with others as being immensely important is a unique gift. However, it is crucial to use that gift wisely and find the best way to use your gift to suit your particular personality. Serving others is a good thing but it is important to maintain a balance between serving others and being used. Protecting yourself from becoming a complete people-pleaser who cannot say 'no' to anybody or anything, whether it's good for you or not, is crucial to maintaining your personal wellbeing. Learning to say 'no' to injustice and unfairness will help you ensure that people do not take advantage of your giving and serving nature. People with dominant interdependent self-construal may find enjoyment in vocations that allow them to be of assistance to a customer, a manager, a client, or a team. Aligning your personality with your gift or your heart's desire, coupled with determination to reach your destiny and persistence makes living a fulfilling life an inevitability.

Individuals with dominant independent self-construal may emphasize being different and separate from everyone else but they also need interpersonal relationships. If you have dominant independent self-construal, you are likely to use those interpersonal relationships to make progress toward achieving your goals and asserting your individuality. Your main concern is your own achievement, and many relationships with others may be seen as just a means to an end. Much of the time, these relationships are used to make comparisons that reinforce your uniqueness. You will make choices about which relationships to enter into and maintain based on their potential benefits. Within these interpersonal relationships, you are less likely to adapt your behavior or manage your emotional responses to others for the sake of 'keeping the peace.' Your emotional responses tend to be what is called 'ego-focused.' These emotional responses focus on what you are feeling as opposed to focusing on what others are feeling. For example, take the same situation above where your behavior was called out. You are less likely to take on their perspective, emphasize your feelings over theirs, and feel angry at your individuality or the pursuit of your goals being questioned. You are also less likely to alter your behavior going forward to avoid possible future conflict.

People with dominant independent self-construal often do well in leadership positions due to their strong self-perception and high self-esteem. Having independent self-construal is a good thing but it's important to keep yourself in check. Too much of anything is never a good thing. They could well end up being self-centered and selfish, disregarding the feelings, desires, and needs of others. It can be difficult to change how these people perceive themselves and others due to the dominance of their independence. They only value and understand their own perspective on things. If you observe yourself disregarding others, it is important to change the way you perceive and treat others to develop better interpersonal relationships. One of the best ways to tell whether your independent self-construal is becoming detrimental to your interpersonal relationships is if you experience numerous fallouts within close relationships. Nobody can change your perception but you. Constant fallouts within interpersonal relationships may prove to be a stumbling block on your path to success. You need good relationships for your happiness and to be able to work well with others. Even though you are fully capable of achieving your goals, no man is an island.

To change the way you perceive others, think about your behavior toward them and what it's like to be in their shoes. Ask yourself, 'Would I want to be treated this way?' If your answer is 'no,' it may be time to check yourself and bring your ego down a few notches to a healthier level.

Self-Conciliation and Self-Construal

Learning to effect change and be who you really want to be isn't an easy task, but it's worth it. Self-conciliation is linked to self-construal. You cannot make peace with yourself and learn to change what needs changing unless you understand who you are right now. Once you understand who you are in the present moment and what makes you tick, you'll have the necessary insight to determine what needs changing and figure out how to change it. Let's look at a basic model for self-conciliation.

Acknowledge

The first step to self-conciliation is to acknowledge who you are right now, that you are not happy being that person, and that you have the power and responsibility to change. Once you have acknowledged these things, you have no excuse not to make changes. You are no longer a victim trapped within yourself. You are empowered by self-knowledge and can now take action to become who you really want to be.

Let Go

Once you have acknowledged who you are and how you identify yourself, it's time to let those old self-perceptions go. Holding onto self-perceptions and beliefs that don't align with who you want to be, only prevent you from realizing your full potential to live a fulfilling life. Letting go may involve:

- Changing how you see yourself.
- Changing how you think about yourself, others, and the world around you.
- Letting go of the past, whether it's a failure or a negative experience.
- Letting go of a negative mindset and thought patterns.
- Letting go of unhelpful relationships.

You need to redefine yourself in terms of who you want to be and align your thoughts and behavior according to what they should be to allow you to grow into who you want to be.

Reinvention

The final step of self-conciliation is reinventing yourself. You must gain new self-knowledge by practicing internal reflection. Reflecting on yourself brings to light your individual value, your uniqueness, and allows you to discover your strengths. Self-discovery from a positive perspective improves self-esteem, self-perception, and self-efficacy.

4

FACING OUR FEARS

Fear doesn't just come in the form of spiders and the boogeyman under children's beds. Fear wears many hats and can be deceiving. You may not even realize that what you are feeling, or thinking is rooted in fear. However, fear often stands in the way of progress, happiness, and fulfillment in life. Improving your self-perception is going to take facing those fears. In this chapter, we're going to take a look at how to overcome certain prominent fears that hold you back from being who you want to be and realizing your full potential.

ASSERTIVENESS

Social intelligence involves two major aspects:

- Sensitivity toward the emotions of others.

- Behavioral skills for appropriate responses to the emotions of others.

Assertiveness is a skill that straddles both of these aspects. To be assertive is:

- Being sensitive toward the emotions of others.
- Picking up on the social signals others are giving you.
- Understanding the behavior, emotions, and needs of others.
- Responding appropriately to the needs, emotions, and behavior of others.
- Being able to say no.
- Being able to stand by your values, principles, and opinions.
- Expressing yourself effectively.

Assertiveness is not:

- Selfishness.
- Always getting your way.
- Being aggressive.
- Bullying others.
- Manipulation.
- Disregarding the rights of others.

AGGRESSIVENESS VERSUS ASSERTIVENESS

Assertiveness and aggressiveness are often misconstrued as being similar or the same thing, but they are polar opposites. Aggressiveness occurs when you put yourself above anyone else. It is based on the desire to win or get your own way regardless of the costs to others. Aggressive behavior is often selfish and comes across as bullying.

Assertiveness allows you to stand up for yourself while being respectful toward others and their needs and feelings. You focus on finding a balance and facilitate open and honest communication. Assertiveness gives you the confidence to tackle social obstacles in a firm but conscientious manner.

WHAT PREVENTS ASSERTIVENESS?

There are a few things that get in the way of your ability to be assertive:

Fear

The fear of being assertive is often rooted in the desire to avoid conflict or hurting others' feelings. You don't want them to feel bad, get upset, or become angry. You may also fear disconnection from that person by creating conflict or distance between you. You may also fear being rejected by others for asserting yourself.

How do you overcome the fear of being assertive?

- Acknowledge that the fear of upsetting the apple cart in a relationship is universal. Human beings are social creatures that thrive in interpersonal relationships. This creates a natural tendency to want to maintain harmony and avoid exclusion or rejection. This fear of exclusion or rejection is a core fear in the vast majority of people.
- Accept that you have the fear of rocking the boat and take a moment to think about how likely you are to be excluded or rejected, or if you will dramatically hurt or anger the other person.
- Remind yourself that assertiveness is a powerful communication tool that can be used to strengthen relationships, not weaken, or break them. Sharing your views, emotions, needs, and desires with others allows them a deeper insight into you and your relationship.
- Remind yourself that being assertive takes courage and courage only happens when you feel the fear but persevere anyway.

Low Self-Esteem

You may feel that you don't have the right to be assertive. Low self-esteem may be a source of feeling that you don't have the right to express yourself to others or get what you want.

Low self-esteem is the most difficult barrier to overcome when learning to be assertive. The development of low self-esteem is often rooted in experiences from your childhood and past relationship patterns. These experiences are often connected to strong emotions that need to be overcome.

Lack of Skills

You may lack the skills necessary to effectively express yourself. Assertiveness requires the ability to communicate and express yourself effectively. If you cannot appropriately express your thoughts, needs, feelings, or desires in a way that others can clearly understand (and which is neither passive nor aggressive), you cannot be assertive.

A good way to learn how to effectively express yourself is by using 'I' statements. These statements place the focus on you, how you are feeling, and what you need. Using "you' statements easily comes across as aggressive and puts the other person on the back foot by making them feel like they are threatened and under attack.

Example of a 'you' statement:

> 'You make me sad when you go for a boys' night out without telling me. You make me feel unimportant. Why can't you just tell me?'

Example of an 'I' statement:

> 'I feel sad when you go for a boys' night out without telling me because I feel like I am unimportant to you. It would mean a lot to me if you would let me know you are going on a boys' night out beforehand.'

Can you see how the 'I' statement takes the emphasis off what the other person is doing to upset you, and instead places the focus on what you are feeling? This way of expressing yourself is assertive, respectful, and doesn't put the other person on the defensive.

WHY IS ASSERTIVENESS IMPORTANT?

Being able to be assertive is a vital skill that is necessary for healthy, fulfilling interpersonal relationships.

Negotiation

Being assertive allows successful negotiation to take place and mutually beneficial solutions to be found. Being assertive is not about being a bully and disregarding other. An assertive person is able to value their own position as well as see, understand, and value the other person's position. They are able to effectively work with them to come to an agreeable solution to a problem.

Leadership Skills

Assertive people make great leaders by being respectful and fair. Learning to be assertive is a valuable leadership skill that earns the respect of others, even if they may not necessarily like some of the decisions made.

Anxiety and Stress

Assertiveness brings with it confidence and empowerment. Situations are handled without unnecessary stress or anxiety from feeling threatened or victimized. Being assertive means being decisive and developing critical thinking skills to help face challenges when plans don't work out the way they were envisioned.

Problem-Solving

Assertive people don't feel powerless or hopeless in the face of challenges. They feel confident and empowered to do whatever they need to do. This feeling of power allows them to think creatively to find the best solution to a problem or situation.

Confidence

Being assertive takes confidence but it also increases confidence along the way. The more often a person is able to successfully assert themselves with favorable outcomes, the more confident they are in their abilities and problem-solving.

Recognizing Your Emotions

When people allow themselves to be treated like doormats and let others walk all over them, they are likely to suppress their emotions. When people are aggressive and bully others into conforming to their demands, they may be masking deeper emotions. Being assertive helps reflect on thoughts and emotions. It also develops better recognition of those emotions, providing a deeper understanding of self.

Communication Skills

Learning to be assertive means learning to communicate better. Assertive people are effective communicators and being assertive helps them hone communication skills. In this case, effective communication means having the ability to actively listen to others in order to understand and appropriately act on what others say. Assertiveness allows you to communicate your concepts and ideas effectively so that they are heard and properly understood.

Effective communication skills can be learned and adapted. How well people understand you will help determine the effectiveness of your communication skill.

- Does your word use and the way you speak to others cause you to have many fallouts with people?
- Do others regularly take offense when you try to pass on information or explain yourself?
- Do people always seem to go against your advice?

If you answered 'yes' to any of these questions, it may be time to reevaluate the efficacy of your current communication skills. The reactions people have to your communication may indicate how effective your communication is. Having poor communication skills makes it difficult to be assertive. Therefore, you need to work on improving your communication skills if your communication is not effective. Communication skills can be improved by training yourself with the aid of various tools, such as books about how to communicate effectively.

Relationships

Far from being detrimental to relationships, assertiveness enhances and improves them by creating equality, open communication, fostering honesty, and finding a middle-ground during the conflict. It aids in building healthy, happy relationships.

Satisfaction

Assertiveness allows people to get what they want, within reason. They are able to express their needs, desires, and feelings to others and stand by their beliefs and opinions. If what they want is fair, being assertive helps them achieve those goals, which increases overall satisfaction.

HOW TO BECOME MORE ASSERTIVE

Assertiveness isn't something you're born with — it is something that is learned. Lacking assertiveness now doesn't mean you can never be assertive. It's not easy to learn to be assertive when you're not accustomed to it, but it's not impossible and you can do it.

You and Your Rights

You have the right to have a voice, an opinion, an idea, a need, or a desire. You have constitutional rights. You have the right to be treated with fairness and respect. You have the right to be assertive. The first step toward becoming more assertive is to value yourself and your rights. If you don't value yourself and your rights, you will not find the courage to stand up for them.

You and the Rights of Others

You are not the only one who has rights. Asserting yourself in defense of your rights is one thing. Disregarding the rights, needs, wants, and feelings of others is not in the cards when it comes to being assertive. Assertiveness requires you to treat others with fairness and respect. Their wants, needs, rights, and feelings are just as important as yours.

When making requests for your needs and wants to be met, ensure that you are not infringing on someone else's rights, sacrificing their needs or wants, or in any other way disregarding them. Not only will they be less likely to comply or negotiate, but you could also end up damaging your relationship beyond repair.

Express Yourself Confidently

Living a fulfilling life requires your needs and wants to be met. When they are met, you are able to realize your full potential. Waiting around for others to recognize your needs isn't going to get you anywhere. Others may never realize what you want or need if you don't tell them.

Learning to express yourself openly, honestly, and confidently will allow you to communicate your needs and wants to others. You can tell others what you need or want from them to help you lead a contented life, achieve goals, and more.

Don't mistake confidence for aggression. Being confident doesn't mean making demands in a pushy way. Communicating with aggression is likely going to turn people off from wanting to provide you with what you want or need. Confidence will help you stick to your guns and make requests or express opinions in an assertive, respectful, and polite way.

Positive Expression

Some issues are difficult to deal with and are inherently negative. However, how you express yourself in those situations is vitally important. The assertive expression needs to be sensitive to the needs, wants, and feelings of others as well as constructive and not destructive.

When dealing with a problem or difficult issue, look for ways to express yourself in a positive way. Focus on the positive aspects, such as a positive solution, rather than the negative aspects. Use positive expressions for negative emotions, such as anger. Avoid destructive behavior and communication, such as unhelpful criticism.

You Cannot Control Others

The idea that you can control others is a fallacy. You have absolutely no control over what others think, say, or do. Therefore, you have no control over how others will receive and react to your assertiveness. It is important to acknowledge this and try to avoid reciprocating their possible negative reaction with a negative reaction of your own. The only person you can control is you.

Be sure to assert yourself with confidence, respect for others, and without sacrificing their rights, wants, and needs. When you are confident that your actions and decisions are fair and you acknowledge that the response of others is out of your control, it becomes easier to be assertive without feeling guilty if they respond negatively.

Saying No

Many people mistakenly believe that saying 'no' is an act of selfishness when, in fact, it isn't. Learning to say no helps set healthy boundaries and keep them in place. It can be uncomfortable and hard if you are used to trying to please everybody all the time but being able to say 'no' is a key element of being assertive.

Saying 'no' with a genuine reason is a sign of assertiveness and good self-esteem. However, before responding to others, it is important to have the courtesy to actively listen to them. Considering your priorities and capabilities is the key to successfully responding with confidence and without offering vague explanations or feeling guilty. If a question or request requires some time to think over, simply tell the person that you will get back to them shortly. If you are certain, beyond the shadow of a doubt, that your answer is going to be 'no,' don't hesitate or stall. Provide the answer as soon as you can. Not only is it courteous, but you are also giving the person the opportunity to decide what to do next quicker.

Compliments and Criticism

Nobody likes criticism or negative feedback, but it's an inevitable part of life. If the criticism is fair and justifiable, learn to take it and learn from it. However, that doesn't mean you should take unhelpful, unfair, or unjustifiable criticism lying down. Being assertive means being prepared to stand up for yourself if you don't agree. The important thing to remember is to disagree respectfully and politely while remaining firm.

Positive feedback and compliments, on the other hand, are a pleasure to receive and everybody likes to hear nice things about themselves. The trick is not to allow it to go to your head and accept the positive feedback graciously.

FEAR

Fear is defined as a distressing emotion that arises because of a belief that something or someone is dangerous and is likely to be a threat or cause harm. Fear is something everybody feels; it is a normal part of life. Fear isn't always a bad thing either. Feeling fear is part of survival. Fearing a situation in which you are in danger prevents you from putting yourself in a position that could be harmful or even fatal. However, you don't just feel fear as part of your natural survival instincts. You may feel fear every single day in varying amounts for a wide variety of reasons. Just like fear in survival prevents you from putting yourself in danger, fear may also hold you back from reaching your goals and living a fulfilling life.

It's been suggested that fear is comprised of two parts: emotion and rationality. The problem with fear is that the emotional aspect is more powerful and overrides your rationality. Essentially, how likely the perceived threat really is to cause harm doesn't matter because the emotion is powerful enough to cloud your judgment and rational thinking.

Fear management is the management of the emotions within your fear to help you overcome and move past them, unlocking your true potential. Each person is different, and therefore everybody has different fears. What you fear may not be what I fear and vice versa. You need to figure out what you are afraid of before you can begin to manage your fears.

Record Your Fears

An effective way for pinpointing what you are afraid of is to spend a week recording your fears. Every time you feel fear, jot down what you were afraid of, why you were afraid of it, and what you did in response to that fear. Do this every day for about a week. At the end of the week, you will have a list of fears, the reasons behind them, and a record of how you typically respond to each. This list will provide you with clarity and insight into what you fear, why you fear it, how often you feel fear, and which fears you feel most often.

Tip: Find someone you trust, your steady rock in stormy seas, the person who supports you, and ask them to help you on your fear management journey. Speaking to that person about your fears may be helpful to gain an objective insight and perspective.

Fear is Not Shameful

There is no shame in feeling afraid of something, however irrational that fear may seem. Don't shoot yourself down because other people think the fear is silly. Don't compare your fears to the fears of others. Remember, everybody is unique and will have different fears. Being ashamed of your fear increases your anxiety around that fear as you try to work out a way to not be afraid. The anxiety will cause you to hide your fear from others until you can figure out how not to be afraid. Fearing your fear creates more fear; now you are not only afraid of something, but you are afraid of being afraid of it.

Fear Becomes Amplified

You may find yourself dwelling on your fear, thinking about how to get past it or get out of the situation you fear. This overthinking creates an elaborate prediction of disaster that gives the fear more power over you. Overthinking also creates a more intense fear by replaying the worst possible outcome over and over in your mind. Eventually, what started out as a niggling worry could build up to a panic-inducing, anxiety-triggering fear of monumental proportions.

Fear and Stress

Fear and stress are interlinked. They amplify each other and wreak havoc on your mind and body. When you are stressed, fear can be blown out of proportion and triggered more easily. In this way, stress increases fear. The same thing happens with fear increasing your stress. It can turn into a vicious cycle until you're a nervous wreck.

FEAR MANAGEMENT

There are several ways in which you can learn to manage your fears and lessen the negative impact they have on your life and wellbeing.

Accept Your Fear

The first step to managing fear is to accept that it exists. Your emotion is very real, irrespective of whether the threat is real or not. Your fear isn't going to magically disappear. You're not going to feel unafraid of what you fear. What you can do is manage that fear.

Find the Source.

Figure out where your fear comes from. It can be helpful to examine the emotions you are feeling and the concerns you are having more closely to help determine the source of your fear. There are often deeply rooted sources of fear that can be traced back to childhood or dramatically impactful adult experiences. Pinpointing the root source of your fear won't make it go away, but it will provide you with a better understanding of why you are feeling fearful in a particular situation.

For example, you may be worried about confronting someone. Your concern may be that they will reject you because of the confrontation. The fear of rejection may come from a painful experience of rejection you had as a child. You now have a better understanding of why you are fearful of confronting people and where it all started.

Be Specific

Part of identifying the source of your fear is to gather as many details about your fear and emotions as possible. Ask yourself some open-ended questions to help you uncover specific details about your fear.

- Is the outcome you fear likely to happen?
- If you feel it is a likelihood, how likely is it that the outcome will happen?
- If that outcome does happen, how would you respond?

The Five Why Method

You may think that there is only one answer to asking yourself why something scares you. However, you may produce different answers if you ask yourself the question multiple times. Ask yourself why it scares you five times. Every answer you provide gets you one step closer to finding the root cause of your fear. Each answer may also help you find a wider variety of solutions or a solution that will deliver better results.

Find the Facts

Fear is a subjective emotion that can skew your thinking about the rationality of that fear. Gathering certain facts can help you figure out how likely an outcome may be or diminish the fear by bringing rationality into the equation.

For example, consider confronting someone about a problem where you fear being rejected by that person. What is the nature of the problem and how big is it? How close are you to this person? What is your relationship with the person? Is the person calm and easy-going or do they have an explosive temper? Answering questions like these may help you determine the likelihood of the outcome you fear rejection. If the problem is small, you are close to them, they are your best friend, and they have a generally mild temperament, then the likelihood of rejection is minimal. Your fear doesn't go away, but it may be lessened by bringing some rational thinking into managing that fear.

Tip: Ask someone who experiences a similar fear about how they feel and how they deal with it for a less subjective perspective on the situation. They may be able to provide you with 'facts' you didn't think of.

Evaluate Your Options

Consider your fear and try to come up with constructive ways to deal with what scares you. Not all your options will be effective at managing your fear, but you should be able to narrow them down to ones that will help you manage or move past your fear.

Tip: It may be helpful to bounce your ideas off that close friend of yours. They might have a more objective perspective, free from the judgment-clouding effect of the strong emotions associated with your fear. They may even be able to come up with solutions you didn't consider.

Do not Avoid

You will never learn to manage your fear if you avoid it altogether. Some fears you can't avoid, but others you can. You will never learn to manage your fear if you avoid it altogether. Avoiding what scares you maintains the fear as an obstacle, and you won't be able to overcome it or move past it.

Gradual Exposure

When facing your fear, do so gently. Diving into facing an intense fear head-first may create an overwhelming experience that solidifies the fear instead of helping you manage it. Gradually exposing yourself to fears helps lessen your anxiety and fear over time through repeated exposure to what scares you.

Put the Past Behind You

Fears can often stem from unpleasant, painful, or even traumatic events in your past. These events left an impression on you that you are carrying around as emotional baggage. This emotional baggage creates a fertile breeding ground for fear and holding onto past experiences allows fear to keep you trapped. In order to face or overcome a fear rooted in your past, you must face your past and let it go. Putting the past behind you can lessen or even help you completely conquer the associated fear.

While both negative and positive past experiences make us who we are, we know that we cannot change the past. However, we do have the power to change the present. Make a point of always using your past experiences to benefit your present and future. Regardless of how bad a past experience may be, as an adult, you have what it takes to control what is happening now and ensure that past experience doesn't happen to you or your loved ones again.

You have the ability to retrain your brain to acknowledge any negative past experience as remaining in the past without defining your present. If you can, make use of your past experiences to help educate and protect others from suffering the same way. Avoid living in the past and harboring feelings of guilt. You cannot change what happened then, but you can change what is happening now.

Follow a Healthy Lifestyle

Anxiety surrounding a specific fear may be managed better when you lead a healthy lifestyle and get enough sleep. When your body is healthy, your brain works better. When your mind is rested, it functions better, and you can think more clearly. A healthy lifestyle also helps reduce stress which, in turn, makes anxiety easier to deal with.

A healthy lifestyle includes:

- Balance your personal and work life so you are not overworking yourself.
- Live within your financial means so you don't incur unnecessary debt, which adds to stress and feelings of guilt.
- Eat a healthy, balanced diet for physical and mental health. When your body is healthy, your mind works more efficiently.
- If you are currently at an unhealthy weight, you have the power to change for your own health and happiness; it's never too late to make positive changes to help yourself.

Look on the Bright Side

Fear and anxiety can amplify negativity. Not only are you dwelling on negative thoughts and experiences, but you may also notice negative things about the world around you more easily. Deliberately noticing positive things around you and prompting positive thinking helps decrease anxiety.

Barbara Fredrickson conducted research that posited that actively and deliberately seeking out the positive broadens your perspective of the world. Widening how you view life, and the world may offer you more options for finding solutions for fear management. Regularly practicing positivity will form a habit and build resilience within you to improve your ability to cope with scary, stressful, or difficult situations. (How to Deal with Fear and Anxiety, n.d.)

Use Visualization

Your mind is a powerful thing. Visualizing yourself in a situation that evokes fear can make you feel fear without being in that situation. You can also ease the difficulty of facing your fear by visualizing yourself overcoming it. It can help make the fear seem less scary. If you can visualize it and believe that you can do it, you can do it.

Develop a Support Structure

Fear may make you feel alone in your struggles. Having a support system of friends and family in place can help you better deal with your fear. When you feel alone, fear can seem overwhelming and insurmountable. Finding support while dealing with your fear offers you confidence and comfort. They may also be able to offer you a more realistic perspective of your fear or help find solutions. Talking about a fear may also help make it seem less scary.

Talking is among the most therapeutic remedies for many of the problems we face in our lives. There is an English saying that says, 'A problem shared is a problem halved.' This emphatic saying is incredibly true. Human beings are social creatures; there are many times we draw our strength and inspiration from our social interactions with others, no matter how dominant our independence may be.

It has to be noted that it isn't a good idea to share every single problem with every person you know. In fact, it is wise to choose your confidantes carefully. Not every person you meet will have your best interests at heart, especially 'frenemies,' or friends who are more like enemies than actual friends. Arming the wrong people with intimate knowledge about your life and the challenges you face could do you more harm than the temporary relief of letting off some steam.

Finding the right person to support you doesn't necessarily mean turning to the person you think is closest to you. Having a confidant that is close to you may be great, but it's not always possible. It is important to find someone you can trust with the intimate workings of your mind, emotions, and life without the fear of being hurt. If you do ever suffer disappointment after sharing a problem with someone, consider it a lesson learned from a mistake and move on from that disappointment. Don't dwell on it and allow it to prevent you from finding support elsewhere. Simply be more careful with the next person you confide in.

My personal experience: I remember a time when a colleague of mine confided in me about her fears. My colleague is British, and while she was a student in the UK, she met a wonderful man. They enjoyed a strong relationship during their time as students and she fell head-over-heels in love with him.

During their relationship, she became pregnant. However, her partner went back to Uganda after completing his studies. She then had a serious dilemma on her hands and didn't know how to handle the problem. She was desperately in love with this man, and she was carrying their unborn child. She was afraid of the idea of raising their child as a single mother, but she absolutely dreaded the prospect of leaving the UK to move to Uganda to be with him.

I thought about the situation, and I asked her one question: 'Why don't you get married so that he may be granted permission to live in the UK with you?'

Asking her this one question made her instantly light up. In a single moment, an outside perspective was brought in, and her greatest problem and fear were solved. She hadn't thought about getting married as a solution to the problem. She made plans and went to Uganda to get married in a simple wedding ceremony. By the time their baby was born into the world, her new husband had relocated to the UK to be with her and his child.

In this instance, I was able to offer my colleague a different perspective that she hadn't previously considered. Talking to others may help you find new solutions to challenges. However, even if the people you talk to can't offer solutions, they can offer you a listening ear, a shoulder to cry on, or a chance to get something that has been bothering you off your chest. Finding someone to support you in any way you need is incredibly important.

Remember, you are not the first person to deal with the life experiences you are going through, the challenges you are facing, or the emotions you are feeling. Working on yourself and putting into practice what I've been speaking about, you will be able to help yourself in any situation. You have what it takes. You can do it.

FACE YOUR FEAR AND DISCOVER WHO YOU WANT TO BECOME

You may feel as though facing a specific fear is impossible. The emotional aspect is so powerful that it can override your ability to think rationally about the situation. However, you can face your fear to loosen its grip on your life. There are a few things you need to improve to help you along your journey of facing your fears.

SELF-ESTEEM AND FACING YOUR FEARS

Self-esteem is a state of mind in which you either feel good about yourself or you feel bad about yourself. It affects how you perceive yourself. Suffering from low self-esteem may make you anxious about making mistakes and letting others down. Various fears are based on feeling bad about yourself, such as having social anxiety and fearing social situations. In order to face fears that are based on low self-esteem, you need to build a better perception of yourself. But how do you do that?

Identify Triggers

Identify situations or circumstances that routinely lower your self-esteem.

Could it be:

- Your body.
- The state of your house.
- Your past.
- Your job.
- Your education.
- How you dance.
- Your earnings.
- Your looks.
- Your friends.

Write down the things that make your self-esteem plummet and be detailed in describing the trigger. Once you have clearly identified and described the trigger, write down how you would like that triggering situation to change so that it would make you feel better. Now that you have a trigger and an idea of how you would like things to be, it's time to think about what you can do about it. Remember, you have what it takes to help yourself live a fulfilling life.

Develop Awareness

Develop awareness of your internal dialogue, beliefs, and thoughts about yourself in situations that lower your self-esteem. How did you interpret the situation, based on facts or irrational ideas that aren't necessarily true? This will help you gain an understanding of whether your reaction is appropriate according to the facts of the matter and whether that internal dialogue is useful to you.

Becoming aware of your thoughts about yourself is of crucial importance. Sometimes you may think the people around you don't care or that they don't like you. You may end up putting yourself down because of what you believe other people are thinking. However, the truth may be far from it. Other people may just be caught up in their own lives and personal struggles, and it may not be about you at all.

My personal experience: I remember a time my internal dialogue about myself led me to feel poorly about myself. I had invited my friend and her husband over to my house for dinner. They never replied to my invitation, nor did they arrive at my house for dinner. I had feelings of rejection because I felt that my friend didn't care about me.

I didn't have to wait long for an opportunity to talk to my friend. I told her that I felt hurt and as if she didn't care about me because she didn't come for dinner and didn't even bother to respond to me. It was then that I learned she and her husband weren't talking to each other at the time. He had never relayed my dinner invitation to her. This conversation was the first time she found out about the invitation.

I was so caught up in my own mind, dwelling on thoughts about how unimportant I was to my friends, and allowing myself to entertain a self-esteem-lowering internal dialogue. It is vital to stop yourself from assuming you know what is going on in other people's minds. It is almost impossible to know what anyone else is thinking unless they have clearly expressed those thoughts to you before.

Challenge Your Thoughts

Challenging your thoughts is an important step toward improving your self-esteem. If your thoughts in response to a situation aren't based on logic or fact, it's time to challenge them. You can train your brain to generate positive thoughts, opinions, and internal dialogue about yourself in any situation. It is one of the single most important and beneficial things you can do for yourself and your well-being. Whenever your mind generates a thought that is meant to put you down. Identify that thought and challenge it so it becomes positive instead. You are essentially turning negativity into positivity. It won't happen overnight, but it will happen. By being aware of your thoughts and constantly challenging negative thoughts and turning them into positive ones, you will retrain your brain with time and practice. Eventually, you will naturally think positive thoughts about yourself and do what's right for you in any situation.

Important note: Challenging your negative thoughts doesn't mean you should ignore your thoughts altogether. We all have thoughts for a reason. So many great things we do begin as a thought. All it means is that you should use your thoughts wisely and not allow them to stand in your way of achieving your goals and living a fulfilling life. Challenging your thoughts means you are taking full control of your mind and not allowing it to block your path. Remember, you are the only person who can control what you think. Nobody else can do that for you.

Adopt a New Mindset

Alter your mindset if it's stopping you from building positive self-esteem. Your self-perception may be based on subjectivity instead of objectivity. Consider the situation objectively and change the way you think about it to interpret it in a neutral or positive way. Focus on positive aspects of the situation instead of negative aspects.

Banish Perfection

Let go of perfection. Each person is unique. Perfection is a subjective notion. What one person perceives as perfection may be an imperfection to another. Once you realize perfection is subjective and not a factual thing, you will realize that perfection, in fact, does not exist at all and you can let go of the desire to be perfect. It is of the utmost importance to focus on doing what is right in that particular situation.

Develop Patience

Have patience throughout your journey. Changing the way you think about yourself doesn't happen overnight. It's a process that takes time and consistent effort. Changing your thoughts will help you improve your self-esteem, but it's an ongoing process.

SELF-EFFICACY AND DEALING WITH YOUR FEARS

Self-efficacy is influenced by self-esteem. As you start building your self-esteem, you will automatically start noticing an improvement in your perceived self-efficacy. Positive self-efficacy creates a belief that you have the ability to face your fears. When you believe you can face your fears and conquer them, it becomes easier to find solutions for dealing with the fear and builds confidence that you will overcome it.

MENTAL RESILIENCE

Mental resilience is also known as mental strength. Facing your fears requires you to be mentally strong but what does mental strength mean? It is your ability to effectively deal with challenges, performing to the best of your capability, regardless of the situation or circumstances. Improving your mental resilience helps you face fears, improve self-esteem, increase positive self-efficacy, and reduce stress. Here is how to improve your mental strength:

- Learn a new skill to boost resilience by increasing your sense of competency and mastery. Learning a new skill further builds resilience by developing a support base. If your fear involves lacking a specific skill or set of skills, do some digging to find out how you can learn those skills. You may be able to teach yourself to master a skill and gain competency from the learning process. This may mean applying for a new job or returning to education for further learning.
- Set and achieve goals to develop your willpower and determination for mental strength. Setting goals that include learning a new skill combines the development of mental strength you get from mastering a new ability with the resilience development that comes from reaching your objectives. You can also bolster resilience by setting goals that allow you to serve others to provide a sense of purpose.
- Look for opportunities for self-discovery in the face of challenges. Facing and overcoming a challenge, such as facing a fear, helps increase your self-esteem and self-confidence. Much of the time, challenges present themselves to provide you with an opportunity to change direction from your current path and follow the right path instead. Always work through any

challenges that stand in your way with determination to overcome them. Use the opportunity for self-discovery to uncover the true you. Build your strength by tackling and conquering the challenges you face.
- Keep things in perspective instead of making mountains out of molehills. Maintain a long-term perspective when facing immediate challenges.
- Focus on the positive and keep a hopeful outlook on life and challenging situations. Expecting a positive outcome reduces dwelling on fear and negativity.
- Maintain a regular self-care routine to improve mental resilience by managing stress.

SELF-CONFIDENCE

Self-confidence is a vital aspect of self-efficacy and facing your fears. It is the attitude you have toward what you are capable of, as well as how you perceive yourself. Self-confidence and self-esteem are closely related. The better you feel about yourself, the more confident you will be. The more confident you are in yourself, the better you will feel about yourself.

Your self-confidence, like self-efficacy, doesn't necessarily have anything to do with your actual ability. It's all about how you perceive yourself. Your perception of yourself is highly subjective, and therefore, when you are not confident in yourself, your perception may actually be incorrect.

Self-confidence is also variable according to the situation. You may have higher self-confidence in certain aspects of your life but lower self-confidence in others. Having succeeded in one area may lead to higher self-confidence in future endeavors, while experiencing failure in another area may lower self-confidence in that particular area.

Here are some tips for building your self-confidence.

- Know your strengths and play to them.
- Acknowledge and reflect on progress. It's easy to overlook what you have accomplished and focus on what you haven't. Always remember to count your blessings and truly appreciate what you have, even if it seems you don't have much. Not acknowledging what you have and what you have accomplished may make it more difficult for you to achieve your goal and appreciate the achievement.
- Make goals realistic and achievable. Setting the bar unrealistically high can lead to lowered self-confidence if you underperform. If you have a large goal, set smaller goals toward achieving that big goal. It's those little baby steps that really matter because, in taking those small steps, you are paving your way to bigger and better things.
- Leave failures in the past and don't dwell on them. It's not healthy for your self-esteem. Past failures aren't a prediction for future events. Failures exist with a

purpose; they help you gain more momentum which will lead you to success. It's hard to succeed without experiencing failure; it is the road to success. Use failures to build your resilience so that whenever you fall, you are able to get up, dust yourself off, and continue stronger than before with increased determination to win.

- Be kind and compassionate to yourself if you experience setbacks. If you think you can do it, don't give up trying. Giving up too soon lowers self-confidence by fostering the belief that you can't do it.
- Avoid making assumptions about yourself. If you find yourself assuming you can't do something, such as facing a fear, without any factual basis of whether you actually can or not, challenge and change that assumption.
- Use positive self-talk and speak to yourself positively about your abilities. Negative self-talk will drag your self-confidence down and power your perceived self-efficacy. Be your own cheerleader and use that voice in your head to encourage you instead of discouraging you.

BAD HABITS

Bad habits are called bad for a reason. They may be detrimental to your health and overall wellbeing. Bad habits also have the ability to increase your stress, anxiety, and fear. A good example of a bad habit increasing these feelings is procrastination. Leaving things to the last-minute increases anxiety and the fear of failure or letting others down. Bad habits can be hard to break, but there are a few tips to help you along the way.

- Identify the cause or trigger of the bad habit. Perhaps it's the presence of someone, a time of day, a place, an emotion, or a preceding event that leads to the bad habit as a response.
- Determine why you want to give up the bad habit and use that as your focus during the process of breaking the habit. Make your reason personal and beneficial to increase motivation.
- Pick one bad habit to give up at a time. Avoid trying to kick multiple bad habits at the same time.
- Prepare for setbacks. Breaking a bad habit is difficult, especially in the beginning. To avoid losing motivation and eventually giving up trying to break the habit, mentally prepare yourself for setbacks. Have a plan in place for dealing with setbacks and the accompanying disappointment.
- If possible, replace a bad habit with a good new habit. For example, you could replace unnecessary online shopping with reading, listening to an audiobook, or learning a new skill.
- Change your environment. For example, if you have

the habit of procrastination and your fear is of failure or letting others down, remove distractions that tempt you to procrastinate.

NEGATIVE EMOTIONS

Negative emotions and how you deal with them can have a great impact on your life. It's easy to shy away from dealing with these emotions because they are uncomfortable. However, avoiding situations that cause these emotions or suppressing them only creates more problems down the line. In fact, poor ability to effectively handle negative emotions could stand in your way of facing your fears.

Some negative emotions that may affect facing your fears include:

- Anger.
- Depression.
- Emptiness.
- Failure.
- Fear.
- Frustration.
- Guilt.
- Helplessness.
- Inadequacy.
- Jealousy.
- Loneliness.

- Feeling overwhelmed.
- Resentment.
- Sadness.

Most of these emotions affect your self-esteem, which is a vital component of facing your fears. You will need to learn how to cope with negative emotions in order to be able to face your fears.

Dealing With Negative Emotions

When you experience them in the correct context, negative emotions are actually a natural, normal, and healthy part of life. However, experiencing long-lasting negative emotions is damaging to your self-perception, perception of others, self-esteem, self-confidence, and overall satisfaction with life. You have the power to cope with, let go of, and prevent negative emotions from becoming detrimental to your happiness.

Bottling your negative emotions up and ignoring them won't make them go away, and it isn't a helpful strategy for dealing with them. In fact, stuffing your negative emotions only causes you to hold onto them, allowing them to poison you from the inside out. Holding onto these emotions leads to dwelling on them and revisiting them in an unhealthy way. This can have a negative impact on your mental and physical well-being.

Understanding your emotions is the first step on the path to dealing with them. This requires internal reflection to ascertain the situations that are triggering negative emotions. Negative emotions generally stem from one of two things:

1. A triggering event that causes you to feel an unpleasant emotion. It is important to recognize the trigger by being aware of your emotions and picking up on instances where you are feeling a negative emotion. Once you are able to identify when you are feeling negative emotions and why you are able to evaluate what is going on and make sense of it. Sometimes your emotions may be caused by having made a mistake. Sometimes all that may be necessary is to offer someone an apology or an explanation if you think there was a misunderstanding. You may also need to tell someone how you feel about the situation.

2. Your thoughts about a situation and how you interpret what happened. Your subjective perception of the situation may cause you to experience it differently to what the facts tell you about what's happening. Check yourself and take a moment to reflect on why you feel the way you do and why you are thinking about the situation the way you are. It may be time to challenge and dismiss negativity in order to move forward, address the issue at hand, or simply embrace it for what it is.

Remember, the purpose of experiencing negative emotions is often to indicate there is a problem that needs addressing. Whether your negative emotions come from a triggering event or your thoughts and perception of that event, there are ways to help you deal with them in a more positive way.

PATH

Using the PATH method while you are feeling a negative emotion may help you handle it better in that moment.

Pause: Don't immediately act on your emotions. Stop yourself from taking action and take a moment to think about everything that is happening. At the onset of a negative emotion, help yourself calm down so you can think more clearly by counting to 10 or even to 100. Always take time to think before taking action to avoid having regrets later on.

Acknowledge: Acknowledge what emotion you are feeling and accept it for what it is. Accept that negative emotions are a part of life. Understand that feeling what you are feeling is an important part of the process of dealing with that emotion.

Think: Once you have identified the emotion you are feeling and accepted it, it's time to figure out how to deal with the emotion by finding ways to make yourself feel better.

Help: Do what you need to do to help yourself deal with the emotion and express it.

Engage in assertive communication with the person who triggered the emotion, if possible, without getting overwhelmed by the negative emotion and having the interaction degenerate into an argument... Be sure to use the 'I' statement method when directly expressing your feelings.

Address a basic need that may be unmet:

- Drink a glass of water.
- Eat a healthy snack.
- Take a nap.
- Go for a walk.
- Take a bath or a shower.

My personal experience: Knowing what triggers your emotional reactions is very important. I realized that whenever I am hungry, I am easily irritated and prone to easily reacting with outbursts. Nobody likes living with a person who has outbursts willy nilly. So, whenever I start feeling angry or frustrated, I check myself. If I am hungry, I immediately get something to eat. I also told my household about this. The moment they hear me raising my voice one of them will pass me a drink or something to eat before I even realize that I'm getting irritated. This has helped minimize unnecessary arguments in my home.

Boost your mood: Boosting your mood with these suggestions may not always be possible at the moment you experience the emotion, but they may help you deal with the emotion later.

- If keeping busy helps you let go of a negative emotion, find a physical activity you enjoy and do it. Look up pictures, videos, or quotes that bring you a sense of joy on the internet.
- Use positive visualization, such as of your happy place or of yourself as the best possible version of yourself.
- Read an inspiring story.
- Interact with an animal.
- Watch a feel-good movie.

Express your emotions in a constructive way:

- Make a list of what you are grateful for.
- Use art to express your emotions.

- Scream into or punch a pillow.
- Allow yourself to cry.
- Press bubble wrap or tear a piece of paper into little bits.
- Vent your feelings out loud or in writing using pen and paper. You can write a letter to the person who triggered the emotion, keep it for a few days, and then discard it by tearing it up and throwing it away. You could also talk to someone about how you are feeling and what caused that emotion; this may be a good way to gain an objective perspective. Ensure that the person you talk to won't rile you up, will maintain objectivity, and will simply be an ear to listen.

Relaxation techniques:

- Breathing exercises.
- Progressive muscle relaxation.
- Guided meditation.
- Using a stress ball or Play-Doh.
- Yoga.

Further tips for dealing with negative emotions include:

- Release stress by leading a healthy lifestyle. Eat a healthy, balanced diet. Get enough sleep. Drink enough water. Do aerobic exercise which releases

chemicals and hormones to reduce stress and boost mood.
- Avoid blowing a situation out of proportion. Do this by avoiding ruminating. Ruminating is when you dwell on and replay negative emotions, thoughts, and experiences in your mind. These thoughts can become so intrusive that they border on obsessive.
- Focus on the facts of the situation. What do you objectively know about what happened that has nothing to do with your personal feelings about it? Be reasonable about what happened and employ rationality to determine whether your emotion is appropriate for the situation.
- Let go of past events and experiences. Dealing with your past is a powerful way of preventing negative emotions from overwhelming you in similar situations in the future.
- Learn from situations that trigger negative emotions by identifying the emotion and what happened to elicit it. Prepare for future triggering events by coming up with positive, constructive solutions for dealing with the situation and the consequential emotions.

6

THE POWER OF CONSTRUCTIVE RELATIONSHIPS

Interpersonal relationships play a vitally important role in your life. Whether you are highly independent with independent self-construal, or incredibly value your relationships with interdependent self-construal, relationships have a great impact on your life.

According to Vivian Zayas, the relationships you have provide you with comfort and happiness. However, whether the person intends it or not, your relationship with them may also be a source of pain and disappointment. (Swift, n.d.)

Stable relationships are associated with benefits for your mental health as well as your physical wellbeing. Unhappy or unstable relationships are associated with negative effects and may well be destructive to your well-being and sense of self.

WHAT ARE CONSTRUCTIVE RELATIONSHIPS?

Constructive relationships revolve around mutual respect, constructive conflict resolution, and support. Mutual respect is the cornerstone of a constructive relationship. If two people do not respect each other, they will not support each other and will not engage in constructive conflict resolution to find the most agreeable solution possible.

Unfortunately, destructive relationships are becoming more and more commonplace in our modern society. Being able to develop constructive relationships is something you learn from a young age. The connections you build with others during your formative years set the stage for relationships during adulthood. However, if you were caught in a cycle of destructive relationships as a child, you may not know how to build positive relationships with others or recognize the difference between the two. Do not fret, though; all is not lost. You can learn how to recognize destructive relationships and build better relationships as an adult.

Constructive relationships improve your well-being by being supportive and improving self-esteem, self-confidence, self-efficacy, and self-perception. They also set a healthier standard for how you allow others to treat you. Within these relationships, all parties involved respect each other and each other's boundaries. Mutual respect leads to mindfulness of the others in the relationship and respecting their opinions, views, rights, and individuality. From mutual respect and support comes constructive conflict resolution. During this type of conflict, the parties involved appreciate each other's perspective, needs, rights, and wants, and therefore seek to resolve the conflict in an amicable way. They utilize good problem-solving skills to find the best possible solution to the problem that benefits everyone involved. In a nutshell, constructive relationships can also be called healthy relationships.

Other characteristics of a healthy or constructive relationship include:

- Effective, assertive communication: People in a relationship should be able to voice their views, needs, wants, grievances, and more in an open and honest way while still understanding and respecting the other person's views, needs, wants, and rights.
- Honesty: Honesty builds and strengthens trust between individuals.
- Reliability: Reliability is interlinked with honesty and trust. If an individual is not reliable and doesn't do what they say they are going to do, their honesty may be brought into question.
- Trust: Trust is an important factor to discourage disrespect and negative emotions such as jealousy and anger. When people trust each other, they give each other the benefit of the doubt.
- Individuality: Nobody in a healthy relationship should compromise their individuality or base their identity on the identity of someone else. Each respects the other's individuality does not try to change them and affords them the freedom to be who they truly are.
- Compromise: People in a relationship don't always get their own way, they respect each other's perspectives and engage in a give-and-take process for coming to a solution where points of view differ.
- Effective emotional regulation: Regulating one's feelings can be difficult when negative emotions are involved. It can be easy to lash out in anger or pain. In

a healthy relationship, people regulate their emotions instead of letting them get out of control and use constructive, positive ways of expressing negative emotions.

- Mindfulness: Constructive relationships use mindfulness to empathize with each other and understand each other's perspectives and emotions without necessarily being told. This doesn't mean you have to be clairvoyant. It simply means trying to think about what the other person may have experienced that caused their emotions and understand that their emotions are valid.
- Encouragement and support: In constructive relationships, people support each other and encourage them to be the best they can be. This includes supporting their goals instead of putting them down and encouraging persistence and determination to reach those goals. In this way, healthy relationships help build each person's self-esteem, self-confidence, self-perception, and self-efficacy.

It is essential to be aware of the nature of the relationships you have with others. You may be in an unhealthy relationship and not even realize it. This may put you in a position of being in great danger. You may have relationships with some people who do not specifically intend to be unconstructive, while there may be others who do so with intent. For this reason, it is important to take an assertive approach and confront some people with whom you have unhealthy relationships. If you confront these unhealthy relationships and no improvement occurs, it's time to put your self-help knowledge into action.

- Is this what you want in a relationship?
- How is the relationship affecting you?
- Are you able to achieve your goals or lead a fulfilling life with such unconstructive people in your life?
- What do you stand to lose if you keep this relationship in your life?
- What do you stand to lose if you remove this relationship from your life?

Weigh the pros and cons of both maintaining the relationship and removing the relationship from your life. Always make the decision that is right for you and your needs. Remember, you are the only person in that relationship who can make the best decisions to help yourself. It doesn't matter what kind of relationship it is. Sometimes people you consider to be your friend will put you down. Do you really deserve that? What are your goals? What is your worth?

INCLUSION OF OTHER IN SELF THEORY

The Inclusion of Other in Self, or IOS, is a theory that forms part of the self-expansion model. It's easy to get overwhelmed by so many complex words strung together in one sentence, so I'm going to break it down for you and explain what it is and why it matters.

Self-expansion is the innate motivation you have to expand yourself or to improve your potential efficacy by amassing resources that will help you reach your goals. We say potential efficacy because the resources make success possible, but the primary objective of self-expansion is to obtain those resources. The self-expansion model indicates that people have the desire to increase their potential efficacy by nurturing close relationships. These closer relationships, in turn, increase resources. How? They offer access to possessions, social support, social networks, and information. Resources may also include identities and perspectives. These are a little trickier to get around. Identity refers to your personal memories and characteristics. Perspective refers to how you view the world. Drawing on someone else's identity or perspective can be influential for achieving your goals. Considering that self-expansion is the motivation to improve your potential efficacy through close relationships, that doesn't mean it's something you consciously do. Most of us don't enter a relationship purely to gain resources, but the potential resources to be gained influence how attractive others are to you.

Part of the self-expansion model is the Inclusion of the Other in Self-theory. Inclusion of Other in Self may sound complicated, but we refer to it all the time in more layman's terms. Have you ever heard someone in a relationship, either romantic or platonic, say, 'We're attached at the hip,' or 'They are my other half,' or 'They are a part of me?' Those are expressions of IOS, or of being in an exceptionally close relationship. So close, in fact, that you start seeing the other person as part of your own sense of self. As relationships develop, the person you are close to becomes central to your daily life, your future, and even to your self-perception.

Relationships have the power to influence your entire perception of yourself from your self-efficacy to your self-esteem. In healthy, constructive relationships, this power is used for mutual benefit. In unhealthy or destructive relationships, it can be used to the benefit of one and the detriment of the other. Considering this power, relationships therefore also have the ability to influence how you make decisions.

RELATIONSHIPS AND DECISION-MAKING

We're not just talking about romantic relationships here. We are talking about a variety of interpersonal relationships, such as romantic partners, family, friends, and even acquaintances like co-workers. All of these interpersonal relationships have the ability to shape the way you think and how you perceive yourself and the world at large. However, how much power you give that relationship to influence you is entirely up to you.

You make all sorts of decisions every day, from minor to intermediate and sometimes even major decisions. Minor decisions may even be made subconsciously without actually having to weigh your options, like brushing your teeth. You also have bigger decisions that don't necessarily have serious consequences, but must take the other person into account, and potentially even require their input or agreement. An example of such a decision is spending a night out with your own friends without including your partner. Note that we say agreement and not approval.

In a relationship between two autonomous people, or two people who are equal in authority and can govern their own thoughts and behavior, decision-making should not depend entirely on the approval of the other. Of course, when making decisions that concern or affect the other person, consulting them and gaining their perspective or simply their acknowledgment is vital to a healthy relationship. It shows mutual respect and consideration toward each other. However, making a decision shouldn't wholly be based on whether or not you have the approval of someone else in an equal relationship.

However, it often happens in interpersonal relationships that one person hands over authority to the other. It's not necessarily a conscious decision. You might not say to yourself or the other person that you are giving them the power to control your life and decisions. It may start out as one person 'laying down the law' and vetoing the other's decision the first time, but eventually becomes habitual. This is why a strong sense of self-perception, self-esteem, self-confidence, and the ability to be assertive is so important. You should be self-assured enough that you don't allow another person in an equal relationship to have authority over you. When this happens, a relationship is no longer equal; it becomes a parent-child relationship where one partner dictates the other's life.

Sooner or later this tendency and allocation of power from one partner to the other will develop feelings of powerlessness and even resentment. These negative emotions sap your self-esteem and even deprive you of the ability to work toward and achieve your goals. Being able to make your own decisions is intimately linked to your self-efficacy and self-perception. It influences how happy you are with the life you are living and in that relationship.

Another way in which relationships influence your decision-making is by making decisions based on what other people think. Before you even have the opportunity to receive disapproval, you make your decision according to what you perceive others will think. These can be decisions about anything and everything, from what clothes to wear to your career choice. You are exchanging power with those around you, from close relationships to society as a whole.

Interpersonal relationships with others have the power to either make you happy or unhappy. There are several factors that influence how much power you give others, one of which is your sense of self when you first enter that relationship. For instance, if you have a strong sense of self to start off with, you are less likely to hand over an unhealthy amount of influence to the other person. If you enter the relationship with a poor sense of self, you are more likely to allow the other person to have much more influence on your decision-making.

You have the right to provide input in decisions that affect you. You have the right to make your own decisions without needing the 'approval' of someone else. Input should be equal and fair in healthy relationships and, where the decision doesn't affect the other person, you should be able to make your own decisions.

In a healthy relationship, input and mutual agreement is very important for decisions that affect both people. However, if the decision doesn't have a negative consequence for the other partner, there shouldn't be unnecessary or destructive conflict. Let's take the example of having a night out with friends. It is important to consult your partner to let them know you intend to go out but not to win over their approval. Even if your partner doesn't agree with the decision, they will accept that they do not control you and that you have the ability to make your own decisions. In an unhealthy relationship, a partner may use emotional and psychological manipulation tactics to force their decision onto you. This is why understanding what makes a relationship healthy and constructive is so important. You will be able to identify unhealthy relationships that are negatively influencing your life and make the necessary changes. You will also start building more positive relationships instead of falling into more unhealthy, destructive relationships.

If you are concerned about your decision-making ability in any interpersonal relationship, you need to examine how decisions are being made across a broad spectrum of matters. It is up to you to change what is detrimentally affecting your decision-making processes and abilities. You may need to sit down and talk to the other person, or you may need to work on yourself to develop your self-perception and confidence to make your own decisions.

Important note: There are two parties in a relationship. While it is important to consider how the other party in a relationship may be affecting your life, it also works the other way around. You must consider how you may be affecting their life. A healthy relationship is all about fairness.

My personal experience: I had the opportunity to go on holiday with my friends. When I told my husband, he reminded me that we have an upcoming family holiday that was already planned, on which we were going to spend a lot of money. Going on holiday with my friends as well as going on the planned family holiday would put us under financial strain. For this reason, I opted not to go on holiday with my friends. It was my responsibility to be mindful of my family's needs and not compromise those needs, even if I very much wanted to go on holiday with my friends. I did not require my husband's permission or approval to go on holiday with my friends. However, to maintain a healthy relationship between myself and my husband, I needed to tell him about the holiday with my friends. We needed to discuss it and come to a mutual agreement. Relationships are based on a principle of give-and-take. You can't only give, but you also can't only take.

FAMILIAL AND SOCIAL SUPPORT

You now know the influence interpersonal relationships have on decision-making. You can either make your own decisions, allow someone else to make them for you, or allow others to influence your decision without knowing whether they will approve or not. However, the influence of relationships on decision-making isn't inherently negative. There is much positivity to be gained from familial and social support during the decision-making process.

Families and close friends often provide some of the strongest influence on decision-making. They certainly have the power to influence how you live your life, which means they are able to influence the decisions you make. However, a lack of positive, supportive influence can be as harmful to your wellbeing as a negative influence.

The support your family and close friends give you is incredibly important for making decisions that allow you to lead a healthy, happy, and fulfilling life. When you have positive support from your nearest and dearest, you benefit in several ways. You gain:

- Improved self-efficacy, self-esteem, and self-confidence.
- More confidence in your decision-making skills.
- Better problem-solving skills.
- Improved motivation and determination to reach your goals.

In a nutshell, when you have positive support from your family and friends, you feel better about yourself, you have better self-belief, and you have the encouragement to reach your goals. What happens when you don't have that support?

A lack of support is not necessarily the same as being put down by the negative input of others. A lack of support can also come in the form of disinterest. You know that having your decisions and aspirations shot down can lower your self-perception and self-belief. The same thing can happen if your family doesn't take an interest in you and offers you no support at all. A lack of support can make you doubt your capabilities, second-guess your decisions, and lower your motivation.

A substantial factor in motivation is familial and social support gained from friends and family. When you receive encouragement, you are more likely to make better, healthier choices and have the motivation to work hard toward your goals. Having the support to back you up increases your determination to overcome setbacks, learn from mistakes, and keep trying. When those who are closest and most important to you believe in you, you are more likely to have a stronger belief in yourself.

SOCIAL MIMICRY AND YOU

It's well-known that mimicry is one of the primary devices for learning in young children. From a young age, children imitate the adults around them. This can be seen in learning to speak, where a child repeatedly mimics the words an adult says. It can also be seen in learned behaviors, such as brushing teeth, where children learn the mastery of any activity by watching and copying what an adult does. However, mimicry isn't only relegated to children. We continue mimicking others into adulthood, and it can have an impact on your self-construal.

Mimicry Defined

What exactly is mimicry? It is the imitation or copying of other people's gestures, postures, speech patterns, accents, mannerisms, emotions, and moods. This is usually unintentional and done on a subconscious level. You probably don't even know you're doing it. An example of adult mimicry in action is adopting the accent or expressions of a different region when spending time there.

Why We Mimic

Why does social mimicry happen in the first place? It comes down to the connection between perception and behavior. You see someone behaving in a certain way, a representation of that behavior is created in your mind, and you become more likely to adopt or engage in that behavior as well. The reason behind being more likely to engage in that behavior stems from the mental representations created. When you perceive a behavior, that mental representation overlaps with the mental representation that is created when you engage in that same behavior. The creation of one representation leads to the creation of the other.

Mimicry is important in a social context. You are more likely to mimic those around you when you have the desire to engage with them. Once you want to interact with someone you mimic them in various aspects in a bid to get them to like you. The more you want that person to like you, the more you mimic them.

There are several social contexts that influence social mimicry and the extent of the mimicry.

- Peers are more likely to be mimicked because of the ability to identify with them.
- People who have been ostracized are more likely to mimic the person who ostracized them to win them over again.
- Subordinates are more likely to mimic the authority figure above them.
- People may even engage in mimicry if they feel too disconnected or separated from others.

Your propensity for mimicry may also depend on your personality. Some people are naturally more inclined to mimic others based on their self-construal. A person with dominant interpersonal self-construal places exceptional value on their social connections. They want to be affiliated with their social group and are therefore much more likely to mimic others. For people with dominant independent self-construal, social connections aren't high on their priority list. They are less interested in being affiliated with social circles and are less likely to engage in social mimicry.

Social mimicry helps you adjust to your environment in a social context. Being able to self-monitor your public image and adjust to your social surroundings makes you more inclined to be adaptable by mimicking the person or people you are interacting with. If you're not motivated to 'fit in,' you are less likely to mimic the people you are interacting with. You'll be less adaptable to your environment and more likely to 'stand out.'

How Does Mimicry Affect Relationships?

- The person doing the mimicking comes across as more likable to the person being mimicked and interactions are therefore more pleasant.
- The person being mimicked is often more helpful to the person doing the mimicking.
- The person being mimicked feels closer to others and is more likely to engage in social behavior that benefits others, such as volunteering or making donations.
- By mimicking someone, the mimicker adopts attitudes and preferences and experiences emotions similar to the person being mimicked.
- Mimicry may even begin to alter self-construal, especially when self-construal is linked to the society or culture you live in. Despite your current self-construal, you may lean more toward the self-construal encouraged by the society around you.

To sum it up, unconscious social mimicry may aid in developing smoother, more constructive relationships over time. You align yourself with those around you to a greater degree. This leads to higher social acceptance and social support. As we mentioned earlier, social support can be a powerful tool for helping you reach your goals and leading a happy, fulfilling life. For this reason, social mimicry can be of great importance. However, if overused, you may lose your sense of self in your bid to align yourself with others. If this mimicry is based on bad influences, it could be detrimental to you.

THE GOLDEN RULE

You may not know it by its name: the golden rule. However, you already know the concept behind it. It is a moral concept that suggests that you should treat others in the way you yourself want to be treated. It's a principle that has been encouraged by numerous societies, cultures, and religions over time. It is there to help increase the smoothness of interpersonal relationship interaction, and therefore, improve overall life satisfaction.

The golden rule can be interpreted in three main ways:

Positive: In this form, the golden rule is used in a positive sense to direct you to treat others in the same way you would wish to be treated.

Negative: In this form, the golden rule is used in a negative sense to prohibit you from treating others in a way you, yourself, would not want to be treated. An example would be not treating others unkindly if you don't want to be treated unkindly.

Empathic: In this form, the golden rule goes beyond simply your words and actions, it enters your thoughts. It states that you should only wish upon others what you would wish upon yourself. An example would be only wishing good for others because you only wish good for yourself.

These may be different iterations of the golden rule, but they all come down to the same concept. The concept is meant to be a guideline for learning to treat others better by using how you want to be treated as an example.

The golden rule may help you enhance relationships and minimize interpersonal relationship conflicts. Employing the principle can make you more mindful of others and help you regulate your emotions and emotional responses more effectively.

7

THE NEW ME

> "I, not events, have the power to make me happy or unhappy today. I can choose which it shall be. Yesterday is dead, tomorrow hasn't arrived yet. I have just one day, today, and I'm going to be happy in it."
>
> — GROUCHO MARX

You may have heard it many times, so many times, in fact, that it may have lost its meaning by now: 'Live in the moment.' This single phrase has truth within it that resonates deeply with those who embrace it. Rediscovering and reinventing yourself to lead the happiest and most fulfilling life possible starts with living in the present.

The past is in the past. Holding onto negative past experiences only leeches the potential out of this current moment. Living in the past also affects your future in that what you believe happened in the past is what you believe will happen in the future. Clinging onto the past also makes you fearful of and worry about the future.

The future isn't certain. It hasn't happened yet and there is no way to tell what it holds in store. Focusing on the future distracts you from the now which can steal joy from the present and make you overlook or miss out on opportunities as they come by. Constantly looking to the future prevents you from grabbing today with both hands and making the most of it.

Dwelling on the past and focusing on the future leads to overthinking, the amplifier of fear, and the perpetuation of poor self-efficacy. Everything you have learned in this book so far has led you on a journey of discovery. You want to change, you have the power to change, and now it's time to put it all together to transform into the new you. But before that can happen, you have to learn to live in the present moment.

OVERTHINKING: YOU AREN'T YOUR THOUGHTS

Overthinking is a trap that keeps you stuck in a cycle of negativity. When you constantly overthink everything, your mental and physical well-being suffers. You are unable to work on yourself and improve yourself to become the person you really want to be.

How often do you wish you could escape the pressures of your daily life and daydream of taking a vacation? How often, when you finally do take that vacation, is your time spent worrying about the pressures you escaped and left behind? How often do you ruminate, almost obsessively, about negative past experiences for fear of them happening again or because you're holding onto past hurt? How often do you worry about the future or spend time fantasizing about future successes instead of working toward achieving those future desires today?

According to Buddhists, our minds are like monkeys, swinging from tree to tree. Taken in a more figurative sense, it means our minds aren't able to appreciate the present because they are constantly swinging from one thought to another. We allow our thoughts to control us and run rampant with us instead of being mindful of the present. Mindfulness refers to being fully present in the here and now, mind and body. It means bringing stillness to a jumbled, frantic mind and intentionally becoming aware of the present.

The value of living in the moment has been acknowledged by millions. Many people want to do it, but they don't know how to. When you are not fully present in this precise moment, you are not in the moment to realize that you are not here. It takes intention and practice to override your distraction reflex and become mindful of the here and now.

Cultivating mindfulness to combat overthinking is a vital skill. You may find that your self-esteem gets a boost, and you are able to accept your personal weaknesses more easily. Acknowledging your strengths as well as your weaknesses helps build positive self-perception and efficacy. Mindfulness enhances relationships by minimizing conflict with compassion, understanding, empathy, and less defensiveness.

Don't Do, Just Be

Constant mindfulness doesn't happen overnight, and it takes hard work to cultivate a constant state of mindfulness. However, mindfulness, in itself, is pretty easy. The challenge is not to set the goal of being mindful for the next few minutes, hours, days, or weeks. You are still focusing on the future. What you should be focusing on is this very moment, not the next one. You should be focusing on being mindful right now, not eventually.

Mindfulness is a bit of a paradox. It is a great tool to use for self-improvement, but it's not about self-improvement at all. It will help you become who you want to be, but the focus is not on going from who you are now to who you want to be. The focus is the present. The New Yorker published a cartoon that perfectly sums up the concept of mindfulness. In this cartoon, there are two monks sitting next to each other, meditating. The younger and less experienced monk is looking at the older, more experienced monk with a puzzled expression. The older monk responds to this puzzled look by saying, 'Nothing happens next. This is it.'

Mindfulness is so easy that you can do it at any moment, even right now. All you have to do is dedicate your full attention to your experience right now. Imagine yourself as nothing more than an observer of the world around you. What is happening at this very moment? What can you feel, physically or emotionally? What can you hear or smell? Draw your attention to sensations rather than thoughts. Irrespective of whether what you are experiencing is pleasant or unpleasant, experience it because it is the reality of your present. You aren't experiencing it and judging it as good or bad; that would require you to think about it, negating the point of being present in the moment. Just be and let what you are experiencing be. Your mind will inevitably start to wander, and thoughts will try to intrude, especially in the beginning. When this happens, gently guide yourself back to focusing on the moment you are living in.

Mindfulness isn't a goal to be achieved. It isn't something to regret not learning or even spend time thinking about. It is simply the practice of bringing your attention to what is happening immediately. Mindfulness is about appreciating and living life to the fullest in the present moment. If you live life mindfully, your future is automatically catered for. The best time to be mindful is now, as doing this will sort out your future. When you are able to experience a moment for what it is — without judgment — without regret about the past or worry about the future — when you are aware of just being alive, you are living in the moment. Nothing happens next. This is it. This is mindfulness.

SELF-LOVE: UNLOCK YOUR BEST LIFE

Self-love is a buzzword that gets sprinkled into countless average conversations every single day. The concept of learning to love yourself or love yourself more is a hot topic these days. Some phrases you may have heard, or said yourself, that suggest self-love is the key to living a fulfilling life include:

- 'You can't love someone else until you learn to love yourself first.'
- 'You need to learn to love yourself more.'
- 'This wouldn't have happened/be the situation if you just loved yourself.'
- 'Why don't you/can't you just love yourself for who you are?'

Self-love is vitally important for becoming who you really want to be and living the life you really want. It is crucial to build and maintain your mental and physical well-being. It influences your self-perception, efficacy, self-esteem, confidence, relationships with others, decision-making, problem-solving, and capabilities of handling stress and challenges. As such, self-love is the key to unlocking your best life and making the most of it.

Self-Love: A Definition

Self-love can also be called self-care. It is not just about feeling good in the moment by doing something that makes you feel good. Self-love is about appreciating yourself for who you are, 'warts and all' as they say. The things that will help you develop self-love are the things that support growth within the physical, mental, and spiritual spectrum of your life.

How to Practice Self-Love

Mindfulness

Unlike the mindfulness we just mentioned for living in the moment, mindfulness for self-love is about knowing what you think, what you feel, and what you want out of life. You can make decisions and take action according to this self-knowledge instead of thinking, deciding, and acting in accordance with what others think or want for you.

Intentional Living

Intentionally live the life you want to live. You may not always know what that means, exactly, but your decisions and actions will align themselves with the purpose you have set for yourself. If your purpose is to find fulfillment in life, you will automatically make decisions and take actions that lead to a sense of personal fulfillment. When you are living in accordance with your intent, your self-love is improved by feeling good about yourself. Establish how you intend to live your life and start living according to that intention.

The decisions and actions we make in life are fundamental for self-love. If you have important goals in life, it is critical that your decisions and actions align with your purpose. People who never follow their intent in life end up living with a lot of regrets.

For example, you may be a person who loves children, and you want to have children of your own. If you marry a person who makes it clear they do not like children and never will have children, you may give up your desire and intent to have children for the love of your partner. However, chances are you will always feel unfulfilled and feel like there is a void in your life that nothing else can fill.

Sacrifices like these, giving up your intended purpose in life, may lead to major conflicts within a relationship and inner conflicts with yourself because you are automatically searching for your innate purpose. You don't want to be the person who lies on their deathbed wishing you had lived the life you truly wanted to live.

Self-Forgiveness

It's easy to be overly self-critical. Holding yourself accountable for your actions doesn't mean you should punish yourself for mistakes or disappointments. Accept that you are only human. You don't know everything. You can't do everything. You have strengths but you also have weaknesses. Learn to accept mistakes or failures, learn from them, forgive yourself, and move on. A good way to look at disappointments is to appreciate them as an opportunity for growth. If you have grown because of the experience, then there is no such thing as failure.

Care for Yourself

Make sure that your basic needs are met both physically and mentally.

- Get enough sleep.
- Get enough exercise.
- Eat a healthy, balanced diet.
- Experience healthy social interactions with others.
- Be intimate (physically, intellectually, spiritually, and emotionally). You can provide all these forms of intimacy for yourself. They are basic crucial needs that

need to be fulfilled. If you reach a point where you cannot fulfill all of your intimate needs for yourself, you reach a state of self-crisis. When this happens, you need to seek help from your family, friends, or a professional.

Need Vs. Want

Self-love doesn't mean focusing on what feels good. It means focusing on what you need. If that means turning away from something you want because it feels good, then that is what you do. Focusing on what you need rather than what you want helps you find ways to remain strong and find your center, allowing you to move forward. Focusing on what you need helps you break bad habits and behavioral patterns that put your actions on 'autopilot,' which may keep you caught up in the past or get you into trouble in other ways.

Self-Protection

Cultivate relationships with people who are true friends, support you, and are happy for you when you are happy. We all know the term 'frenemies.' It refers to those friends who relish in your unhappiness, pain, or loss. You may even have members in your family who do the same. They are toxic and break down your self-love. It's time to take a closer look at your relationships and decide which ones are good for you and which ones aren't. Cutting loose from harmful relationships will help you appreciate yourself more.

Set Boundaries

Setting boundaries is an important aspect of self-love. You are prioritizing your own well-being and not allowing others to tear you down or take advantage of you. Boundaries are limits you put on how you interact with yourself and others or how you allow others to interact with you. This can involve learning to say 'no' to a variety of things from overworking yourself to overtaxing yourself for the sake of a relationship to activities that may in some way cause you physical, mental, emotional, or spiritual harm.

You aren't going to miraculously be filled with self-love the first time you do any of these things. It takes time to build and nurture self-love. It is a journey of self-discovery and self-development. By following these steps to improve your self-love, you are taking steps toward making the most of your life by starting to appreciate yourself. It doesn't matter what life throws at you. If you love yourself, you can handle anything.

Important note: Self-love is not the act of being selfish. It is being full of self-love, that the love flows to your neighbors. It will not stop people from treating you the way they choose to, but it will help you to maintain a healthy self perception regardless of how others treat you. Self-love is your key to genuinely loving others because you are able to truly love yourself.

SELF-DISCIPLINE

Self-discipline is a crucial skill necessary for finding fulfillment and happiness in life. According to Wilhelm Hoffman (2013), those of us who have high levels of self-control are happier than our peers who have low levels of self-control. During his study, he discovered the reason behind this finding was that those with high self-control, or self-discipline, were able to deal with goal conflicts better. He found that individuals with high self-control:

- Spend less time trying to decide whether or not to behave in ways that are bad for their health.
- Are able to more easily make positive decisions.
- Didn't allow emotions or impulsiveness to influence their decisions.

- Made decisions based on being well-informed and rational.

What is Self-Discipline?

Self-discipline is your ability to govern yourself, work hard, or behave in a certain way without someone else having to tell you to do it. Self-discipline isn't something you're born with; it is a skill that you learn. As such, developing self-discipline takes time and practice. You need to repeat the disciplined behavior until it becomes habitual.

Why is Self-Discipline Important for Happiness?

It's easy to think that mentioning self-discipline and happiness in the same sentence is an oxymoron. After all, self-discipline is often associated with self-denial. A typical example is dieting. Dieting is associated with self-deprivation; you are pursuing the goal of weight loss by 'depriving' yourself of calorie-laden foods. However, is self-discipline really all that bad, and does it make you miserable? The research definitely indicates the opposite. So, why is it that self-discipline comes with a negative connotation?

The reason behind the potentially negative connotation when it comes to self-discipline might be how you perceive it. Take the example of dieting. It takes work and effort to resist the temptations of junk food and stick to a regular exercise regime. You are focusing on the effort and work you have to put into rather than the satisfaction and benefits you will receive from it. Focusing on the negative imparts a negative feeling. Changing your mindset about self-discipline to focus on the positive results that come from exercising self-control will help you develop a more positive attitude toward building self-discipline.

Let's face it, self-discipline takes work and effort. The misconception exists that work and effort aren't pleasant, and happiness is synonymous with achieving pleasure without having to put in any work and effort. If you look at happiness and self-discipline in this way, you need to change your perception of the two. What is happiness, really? Is it the instant gratification you get from the pleasure that requires no effort? No, happiness is not the absence of work, but it is the absence of negative or unpleasant emotions.

Self-discipline shifts your focus from momentary pleasure now, which may have unpleasant emotional consequences later, to a long-term, big-picture view of life. It also inherently sets you up for success and happiness through behavior that avoids situations of temptation and creates healthy habits.

People with high levels of self-discipline proactively avoid situations that are problematic, cause goal conflicts, encourage bad habits, allow distractions, put temptations in their path, or are in any other way bad for them. Essentially, they are establishing happiness by avoiding situations that may have negative consequences. Let's go back to the dieting analogy. Having self-discipline doesn't only mean resisting a cupcake when offered. It also means not going into a bakery while you are on a diet, avoiding the temptation to buy a cupcake. A more positive spin on it would be developing the habit of leaving for work early to avoid putting yourself into a situation where you could arrive late.

How to Develop Your Self-Discipline

Since self-discipline is a learned skill, even if you don't have much of it right now, you can learn to improve and develop your self-control to enhance your happiness.

Find a Reason

Why would you want to work on developing self-discipline if you don't have a reason to motivate you to put the effort in? Find a reason to be disciplined and make it a good one. The more compelling your reason, the harder you'll work to make self-control stick.

Remove Temptation

Self-discipline involves removing temptation or avoiding situations that have the potential to cause negative emotional responses. If you are on a diet, remove temptation by removing junk food from your home. If you have the tendency to get distracted while working, avoid social media and other potential distractions while you are at work. To reach your goals, avoid behaviors, distractions, relationships, or anything else that could steer you off course.

Develop a Routine

Routines bring structure and order to your life and help create good habits. Routines help bolster your happiness because the structure they provide offers a sense of comfort and safety. They also offer an element of predictability in life. You know what you are doing, when you are doing it, and how you are doing it. Following the same routine regularly eventually becomes habitual and soon enough you won't even have to think about sticking to your routine.

Indulge in Self-Care

Self-care is a vital part of maintaining a routine and high levels of self-discipline. Eating healthily, getting regular exercise, and sleeping enough helps keep your mind ticking efficiently. When your head is clear and your body is healthy, you are able to make the right decisions more effectively and easily. Taking time out for yourself as part of your self-care will help you manage your stress, further decluttering your mind of negativity.

Tackle the Important Tasks First

Every day has its own to-do list. That list will have tasks on it of varying importance. As you go through your day, you will find that your willpower, energy, and determination are at their peak at the start of the day. As the day progresses, they may decrease, which may lower your self-discipline. Getting the most important tasks out of the way first prevents you from wasting precious time on the smaller tasks, some of which could even be carried over to the next day if you simply run out of time. The added bonus of completing the most important tasks early in the day is that it creates momentum and motivation that continues throughout the day.

Start Small

Building self-discipline doesn't happen overnight and trying to go from zero to becoming a self-discipline master all at once sets you up for failure. Start small, make tiny adjustments to improve self-discipline, and work your way up to full self-control. Success in achieving a single self-discipline goal creates motivation to achieve the next. Experiencing success also creates momentum to keep you going.

Keep Your Eyes on the Prize

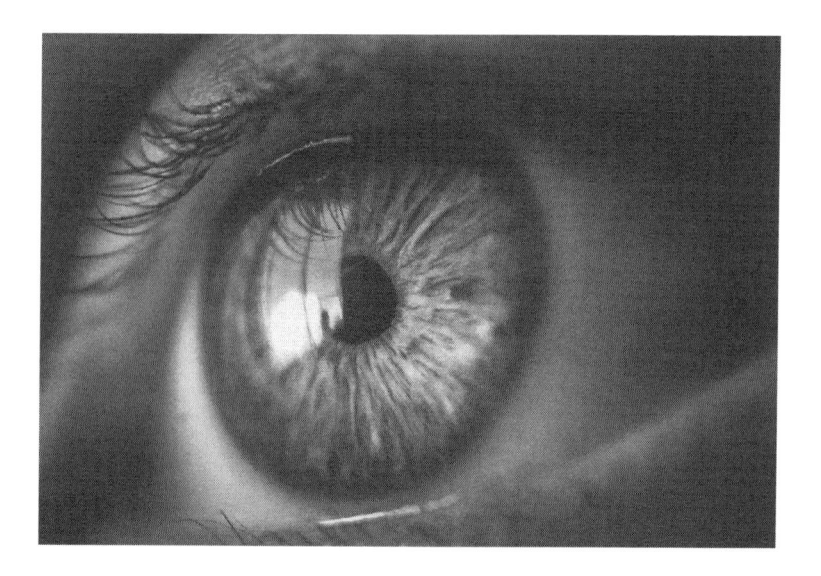

Self-discipline takes effort and dedication. In a world of instant gratification, developing and maintaining self-discipline may seem like a daunting task. To keep yourself motivated to stay disciplined, remind yourself of the reason you want to develop your self-control. Keep your desired end result in mind.

CONCLUSION

Change starts with a simple action: acquiring knowledge and understanding. I have provided you with the knowledge necessary to understand human nature and nurture that will help you gain a far greater insight into who you are now and who you really want to be. You have discovered what is actually standing in your way of achieving success and fulfillment in life despite doing everything you think is necessary. Now it's time to do what is really necessary to make your dreams and aspirations that seem impossible a reality.

Being happy, experiencing good vibes, and leading a fulfilling life is possible. The only thing you have to change is your beliefs about yourself. I've given you practical advice and actionable steps to transform your life by changing how you perceive yourself. Now that you understand what self-belief is, where it comes from, and how it influences your life and your success, you can go about improving your self-perception. It takes time, so don't hesitate. Start making the necessary changes today. There is no better time to start living, believing in yourself, and loving yourself than right now.

I have managed to change my life and you can do the same for yourself. You have what it takes, and you deserve the happiness that will naturally come with that transformation. It's never too late to become 'the master of your own universe' and 'change your stars.' It's never too late to start living a life that is free from regret. The 7 Vital Self-Check Health Program has provided you with the knowledge and understanding. Only you can take action to adapt to habits that will unblock failing relationships, self-love, and self-discipline to achieve good vibes for a fulfilling lifestyle. What are you waiting for? Start building a better, happier you today!

"Start by believing in yourself, then do what is right coupled with everything possible. Suddenly, you are achieving the impossible."

— JONRY HEYCE

If you enjoyed reading this book and found it helpful in achieving success, attracting good vibes, and finding fulfillment in your life, why not recommend it by leaving a review on Amazon?

REFERENCES

5 ways to manage fear. (2020, April 19). Maureen Electa Monte. https://maureenmonte.com/5-ways-to-manage-fear/

AbsolutVision. (2017, November 27). Smiley emoticon anger angry anxiety emotions. Pixabay. https://pixabay.com/photos/smiley-emoticon-anger-angry-2979107/

Alexas_Photos. (2019, May 6). Nobody is perfect motivation overhead projector. Pixabay. https://pixabay.com/photos/nobody-is-perfect-motivation-4393573/

Anemone123. (2017, June 27). Team spirit cohesion teamwork together generations. Pixabay. https://pixabay.com/photos/team-spirit-cohesion-teamwork-2448837/

REFERENCES

Anemone123. (2017, September 10). Question question mark survey problem test. Pixabay. https://pixabay.com/photos/question-question-mark-survey-2736480/

Assertiveness in relationships. (n.d.). Skills You Need. https://www.skillsyouneed.com/ips/relationship-assertiveness.html

Bandura, A. (1994). Self-efficacy. In V. S. Ramachaudran (Ed.), Encyclopedia of human behavior (Vol. 4, pp. 71-81). New York: Academic Press. (Reprinted in H. Friedman [Ed.], Encyclopedia of mental health. San Diego: Academic Press, 1998).

Bniique. (2020, May 31). Eyes look face eye cat girl woman portrait. Pixabay. https://pixabay.com/photos/eyes-look-face-eye-cat-girl-5248678/

Brennan, D. (2020, November 23). Signs of low self-esteem. WebMD. https://www.webmd.com/mental-health/signs-low-self-esteem

Characteristics of healthy and unhealthy relationships. (n.d.). Youth.gov. https://youth.gov/youth-topics/teen-dating-violence/characteristics

Cherry, K. (2020, July 22). Self-efficacy and why believing in yourself matters. Verywell Mind. https://www.verywellmind.com/what-is-self-efficacy-2795954

Davis-Muhammad, M. (2012, September 8). 3 steps to self-reconciliation – Accept yourself. Ezone Articles. https://

ezinearticles.com/?3-Steps-to-Self-Reconciliation---Accept-Yourself!&id=7274183

Ddmitirova. (2015, August 29). Girl father portrait family fatherhood parent. Pixabay. https://pixabay.com/photos/girl-father-portrait-family-1641215/

Delagran, L. (n.d.). How to deal with fear and anxiety. The University of Minnesota. https://www.takingcharge.csh.umn.edu/how-deal-fear-and-anxiety

Dixit, J. (2008, November 1). The art of now: Six steps to living in the moment. Psychology Today. https://www.psychologytoday.com/za/articles/200811/the-art-now-six-steps-living-in-the-moment

Dougandpetegardening. (2018, January 27). Paper document business composition office writing. Pixabay. https://pixabay.com/photos/paper-document-business-composition-3111146/

Eagly, A. H., Nater, C., Miller, D. I., Kaufmann, M., & Sczesny, S. (2019, July 18). Gender Stereotypes Have Changed: A Cross-Temporal Meta-Analysis of U.S. Public Opinion Polls From 1946 to 2018. American Psychologist. Advance online publication. http://dx.doi.org/10.1037/amp0000494

Escobar, S. (2013, April 4). How relationships affect our decisions (including my own. Your Tango. https://www.yourtango.com/2013169910/how-relationships-affect-our-decisions-including-my-own

Fear Management: An essential leadership skill. (2014, December 2). Linkedin. https://www.linkedin.com/pulse/20141202145850-10572825-fear-management-an-essential-leadership-skill

Firmbee. (2015, May 14). Social media Facebook smartphone iPhone mobile. Pixabay. https://pixabay.com/photos/social-media-facebook-smartphone-763731/

Gerace, A. (2017, July 18). How we think about our past experiences affects how we can help others. The Conversation. https://theconversation.com/how-we-think-about-our-past-experiences-affects-how-we-can-help-others-80190

Geralt. (2014, May 25). Self-love heart diary hand keep forest. Pixabay. https://pixabay.com/photos/self-love-heart-diary-hand-keep-3969644/

Geralt. (2015, April 27). Woman face head hand write glass word letting go. Pixabay. https://pixabay.com/photos/woman-face-head-hand-write-glass-737439/

Geralt. (2017, November 13). Human observer exhibition photomontage faces. Pixabay. https://pixabay.com/photos/human-observer-exhibition-2944065/

Geralt. (2018, March 24). Change new beginning risk road clock street sign. Pixabay. https://pixabay.com/photos/change-new-beginning-risk-road-3256330/

Giacomin, M. (2017, July 13). Springer Link. https://link.springer.com/referenceworkentry/10.1007%2F978-3-319-28099-8_1136-1

Golden rule: Treat others the way you want to be treated. (n.d.). Effectivology. https://effectiviology.com/golden-rule/

Grimes, J. (2014, June 7). Your other half? How close is too close: Inclusion of other in self. Psychology Today. https://www.psychologytoday.com/us/blog/the-inner-voice/201406/your-other-half

Helpful Vs. Harmful: Ways to manage emotions. (n.d.). Mental Health America. https://www.mhanational.org/helpful-vs-harmful-ways-manage-emotions

How to build self-confidence. (n.d.). Reach Out. https://au.reachout.com/articles/how-to-build-self-confidence

Influences on self-perception. (n.d.). Lumen. https://courses.lumenlearning.com/atdcoursereview-speechcomm-1/chapter/influences-on-self-perception/

JacksonDavid. (2020, May 23). Hands hand together prayer community creative. Pixabay. https://pixabay.com/photos/hands-hand-together-prayer-5216585/

Juth, V. Smyth, J.(2010, December 2). How do you feel? Self-esteem predicts affect, stress, social interaction, and symptom severity during daily life in patients with chronic illness. NCBI. https://www.ncbi.nlm.nih.gov/pmc/articles/PMC2996275/

Kennedy, T. (2021, March 2). How to build self-discipline to excel in life. Lifehack. https://www.lifehack.org/articles/productivity/self-discipline-the-foundation-of-productive-living.html

Khoshaba, D. (2012, March 27). A seven-step prescription for self-love. Self-love is an action, not a state of feeling good. Psychology Today. https://www.psychologytoday.com/za/blog/get-hardy/201203/seven-step-prescription-self-love

Live in the moment quotes. (n.d.). Good Reads. https://www.goodreads.com/quotes/tag/live-in-the-moment

Mayo Clinic Staff. (2020, May 29). Being assertive: Reduce stress, communicate better. Mayo Clinic. https://www.mayoclinic.org/healthy-lifestyle/stress-management/in-depth/assertive/art-20044644

Mimicry. (n.d.) Psychology. http://psychology.iresearchnet.com/social-psychology/interpersonal-relationships/mimicry/

Mind Tools Content Team. (n.d.). How to be assertive. Asking for what you want firmly and fairly. Mind Tools. https://www.mindtools.com/pages/article/Assertiveness.htm

Morin, A. (2014, October 3). 6 ways to develop the self-discipline necessary to reach your goals. Forbes. https://www.forbes.com/sites/jennifercohen/2014/06/18/5-proven-methods-for-gaining-self-discipline/?sh=4e0b766c3c9f

Nastya_gepp. (2017, September 13). Two people grown up woman portrait fashion brunet. Pixabay. https://pixabay.com/photos/two-people-grown-up-woman-portrait-3075744/

Negative emotions. (n.d.). Better Health Channel. https://www.betterhealth.vic.gov.au/health/HealthyLiving/negative-emotions

Ottowagraphics. (2020, December 20). Teenager hoodie hand no gesture eyes boy teen. Pixabay. https://pixabay.com/photos/teenager-hoodie-hand-no-gesture-5842706/

Randall-Young, G. (n.d.). Decision making in relationships. Gwen Randall-Young. http://gwen.ca/decision-making-in-relationships/

Raypole, C. (2019, October 29). Hot to break a habit: 15 tips for success. Healthline. https://www.healthline.com/health/how-to-break-a-habit

Recognizing and coping with negative emotions. (n.d.). Johns Hopkins Medicine. https://www.hopkinsmedicine.org/about/community_health/johns-hopkins-bayview/services/called_to_care/recognize_cope_with_negative_emotions.html

Relationships in the 21st century: The forgotten foundation of mental health and wellbeing. (n.d.). Mental Health Foundation. https://www.mentalhealth.org.uk/publications/relationships-21st-century-forgotten-foundation-mental-health-and-wellbeing

Ribeiro, M. (2021, April 15). How to become mentally strong. 14 strategies for building resilience. https://positivepsychology.com/mentally-strong/

Sasint. (2016, February 17). Girl sitting jetty docks boardwalk young woman. Pixabay. https://pixabay.com/photos/girl-sitting-jetty-docks-boardwalk-1822702/

Scott, E. (2020, April 30). How to deal with negative emotions and stress. Very Well Mind. https://www.verywellmind.com/how-should-i-deal-with-negative-emotions-3144603

Self-esteem. (2019, January). Mind. https://www.mind.org.uk/information-support/types-of-mental-health-problems/self-esteem/about-self-esteem/

Self-love and what it means. (2020, February 12). Brain and Behavior Research Foundation. https://www.bbrfoundation.org/blog/self-love-and-what-it-means

Shad0wfall. (2015, September 12). Inspiration motivation life inspirational outdoors. Pixabay. https://pixabay.com/photos/inspiration-motivation-life-1514296/

Shortsleeve, C. (2018, August 28. 5 Science-approved ways to break a bad habit. Time. https://time.com/5373528/break-bad-habit-science/

Siragusa, T. (2020, April 14). Achieving happiness through self-discipline. Medium. https://medium.com/radical-culture/achieving-happiness-through-self-discipline-1318e3c34a5b

Sweetlouise. (2020, March 7). Positive thought useful confidence favorable. Pixabay. https://pixabay.com/photos/positive-thought-useful-confidence-4907261/

Swift, J. (n.d.). The influence of Relationships. Cornell Research. https://research.cornell.edu/news-features/influence-relationships

Szalavitz, M. (2013, June 14. Self-disciplined people are happier (and not as deprived as you think. Time. https://healthland.time.com/2013/06/24/self-disciplined-people-are-happier-and-not-as-deprived-as-you-think/

Teamsoul. (2018, August 23). Joe Dispenza – You are the creator of your own world – Do this one thing to control your mind. Fearless Soul. https://iamfearlesssoul.com/joe-dispenza-you-are-the-creator-of-your-world/

Ten ways to fight your fears. (2021, April 14). NHS Inform. https://www.nhsinform.scot/healthy-living/mental-wellbeing/fears-and-phobias/ten-ways-to-fight-your-fears

The importance of being assertive. (n.d.). Teodesk. https://www.teodesk.com/blog/the-importance-of-being-assertive/

The social self: The role of social situation. (n.d.). BC Campus. https://opentextbc.ca/socialpsychology/chapter/the-social-self-the-role-of-the-social-situation/

The Strive Team. (n.d.). Self-discipline: The key to happiness. The Strive. https://thestrive.co/self-discipline-is-the-key-to-happiness/

Viarami. (2020, July 1). Man woman gender female girl people symbol body. Pixabay. https://pixabay.com/photos/man-woman-gender-female-girl-5355842/

What is self-confidence? (n.d). The University of South Florida. https://www.usf.edu/student-affairs/counseling-center/top-concerns/what-is-self-confidence.aspx

Wikandapix. (2016, September 13). Life scrabble word text brown life. Pixabay. https://pixabay.com/photos/life-scrabble-word-text-brown-life-1662879/

Wikipedia Contributors. (2020, December 17). Self-expansion model. Wikipedia. https://en.wikipedia.org/wiki/Self-expansion_model

Wikipedia Contributors. (2021, May 22). Self-efficacy. Wikipedia. https://en.wikipedia.org/wiki/Self-efficacy

Wikipedia Contributors. (2021, May 7). Self-knowledge (psychology). Wikipedia. https://en.wikipedia.org/wiki/Self-knowledge_(psychology)

Made in the USA
Columbia, SC
07 November 2021